Anna-Brigitte Schlittler, Katharina Tietze (eds.)
Bally—A History of Footwear in the Interwar Period

I0093116

Fashion Studies | Volume 10

The series is edited by Gertrud Lehnert.

Anna-Brigitte Schlittler is an art historian and a lecturer at Zürich University of the Arts (ZHdK) and F+F Schule für Kunst und Design. She has studied art history, history, and philosophy at the University of Zürich. Her research focuses on the history and theory of fashion.
Katharina Tietze is a professor of design at Zürich University of the Arts (ZHdK) and head of the Trends & Identity programme. She studied fashion design at Berlin University of the Arts. Her research focuses on fashion, everyday culture, and identity.

Anna-Brigitte Schlittler, Katharina Tietze (eds.)

Bally—A History of Footwear in the Interwar Period

[transcript]

For Ursula Gut

The pre-print preparation was supported by the Swiss National Foundation

Zürcher Hochschule der Künste
Zurich University of the Arts

SWISS NATIONAL SCIENCE FOUNDATION

Bibliographic information published by the Deutsche Nationalbibliothek
The Deutsche Nationalbibliothek lists this publication in the Deutsche Nationalbibliografie; detailed bibliographic data are available in the Internet at http://dnb.d-nb.de

First published in 2021 by transcript Verlag, Bielefeld

Layout: Maja Siebrecht, Zürich
Cover illustration: Ladies' shoe by Bally, 1942; Historical Archives of Bally Schuhfabriken AG, photo: Manuel Fabritz, © Bally
Figure page 6: Bally ski boot, 1944; Historical Archives of Bally Schuhfabriken AG, photo: Manuel Fabritz, © Bally
Figure page 193: Ladies' shoe by Bally, 1935; Historical Archives of Bally Schuhfabriken AG, photo: Manuel Fabritz, © Bally
Translation: Graham Fallowes, Isabel Aitken, Lance Anderson
Copy-editing: Büro LS Anderson, Berlin
Typeset: Trump Mediaeval LT Std
Printed by Majuskel Medienproduktion GmbH, Wetzlar
Print-ISBN 978-3-8376-5738-8
PDF-ISBN 978-3-8394-5738-2
https://doi.org/10.14361/9783839457382

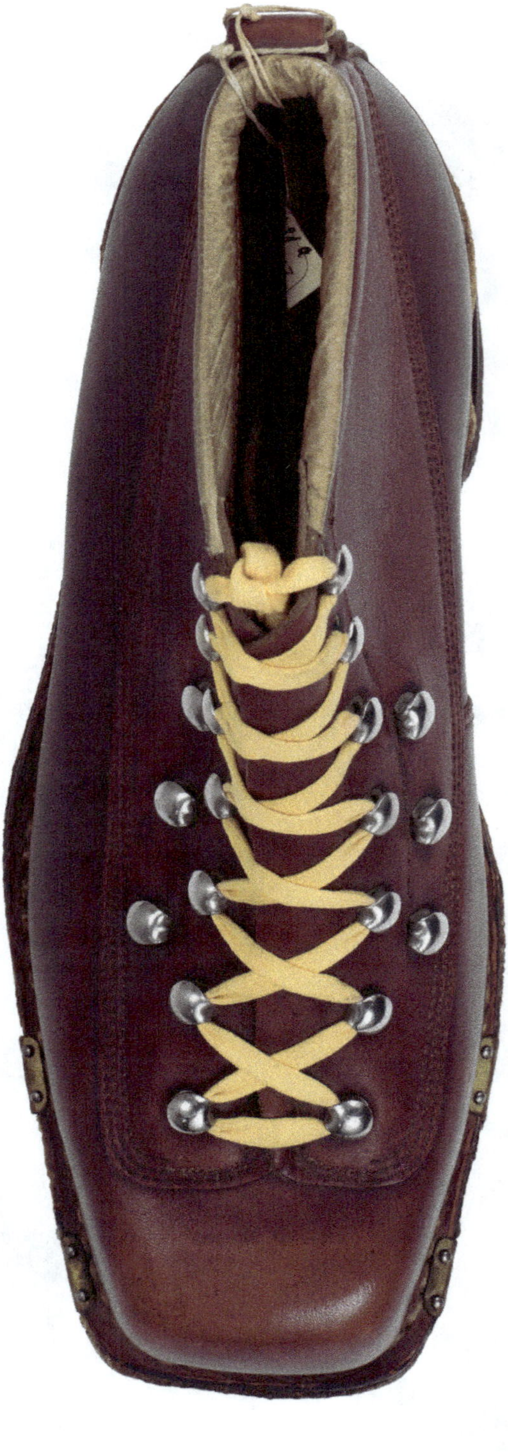

Contents

Introduction

Anna-Brigitte Schlittler and Katharina Tietze

Shoes are accessories. They add the finishing touches to an outfit, complete a look. Shoes offer up information about social identities, class, and gender roles. From clogs to sandals, high heels to brogues, sneakers to boots—shoes have become indispensable extensions of the body, shaping the way we stand and walk. With the appropriate footwear, walking can assume entirely different forms. We might go for a leisurely stroll, a "turn", decide to walk to work, or go for a hike—and so shoes also symbolize our (historically contingent) understanding of public space and our changing relationship to the natural world. At the same time, shoes are also complex, technical products. More than 100 work stages are still required to manufacture classic men's shoes, for example. Nor is the process entirely mechanical or automated. Even today, shoemaking involves skilled crafts(wo)manship. Leather, the most important basic material, should only be cut to shape under the exacting eye of an expert. The evolution of the shoe into a mass-produced consumer product took several decades.[1] Following the development of numerous specialist machines in the late 19th century, production underwent another fundamental change in the first third of the 20th century with the emergence of synthetics and glues. These innovations reduced the number of work stages, which in turn brought down total production costs.

The present work brings together the results of two research projects, both funded by the Swiss National Science Foundation (SNF), on the modern history of the shoe: "Diversity versus Scarcity: Design and Economic Challenges in the Swiss Shoe Industry, 1930–1950",[2] and "Design—Material—Display: The Example of the Swiss Shoe Manufacturer Bally, 1930–1950".[3] The two projects, undertaken in 2013–2014 and 2017–2018 respectively, were coordinated at the Institute for Cultural Studies of the ZHdK—Zürich University of the Arts.

Having served as the starting point for the project, *Bally's* extensive corporate archives yielded an array of diverse historical sources. In addition to thousands of shoes, the archives also contain advertising material, posters, and business documents—sources opened up to academic scrutiny for the first time. Our research focused on fashion design and economic history from the decades spanning 1930 to 1950. This period, which includes the epochal events of the Second World War, witnessed decisive and fundamental upheavals in economic, cultural, and political life. These transformations shaped *Bally's* own history, and shoe design more generally. From the perspective of fashion history, these years stand out for the products' varied design, quality craftsmanship, and technical inventiveness. Shortages during the Second World War precipitated experiments with materials and technical innovations, which reflected developments, both directly and indirectly, in cultural and contemporary history, as well as the unfolding economic situation.

Held in Zürich in 2014, the international conference "Shoes: Design Product, Everyday Item, Research Subject" marked the conclusion of the first project. Contributors' papers were subsequently published as an anthology: *Über Schuhe: Zur Ge-*

[1] The shoe display case at the exhibition entrance, inspired by the view of the design collection in the Bally company archives.
(Exhibition Bally—Swiss Shoes Since 1851 at the Museum für Gestaltung Zürich, 14 March to 11 August 2019, © ZHdK)

schichte und Theorie der Fussbekleidung. Many of the findings from the second project fed into the exhibition *Bally—Swiss Shoes Since 1851*,[4] which was held in 2019 at the Museum für Gestaltung in Zürich [FIGS. I, II] following a proposal outlined by the two editors of this volume.

The economic historian Roman Wild, who was part of the team for the first project, has since been awarded his doctorate. His dissertation was published in 2019 with the title *Auf Schritt und Tritt. Der schweizerische Schuhmarkt 1918–1948* (At Every Step: The Swiss Shoe Market, 1918–1948).

Fashion Studies

In recent years, research on costume history in the field of "fashion studies" has undergone a significant increase in the scope and sophistication of both its content and methodology.[5] This has not been matched, however, by the numbers of specialized academic publications about shoes. The first decade of this millennium saw the publication of seminal publications on the theme, which served to provide important facts, theoretical in-

[II] Installation view of gallery on the company's history. In the foreground, Richard Kissling's bust of Carl Franz Bally.
(Exhibition Bally—Swiss Shoes Since 1851 at the Museum für Gestaltung Zürich, 14 March to 11 August 2019, © ZHdK)

sights, and a selection of methodological approaches.[6] A striking feature of the past few years, however, is the way in which academic studies and exhibitions have developed in parallel to one another. Of course, specific areas of expertise mean that this relationship between museum collections and the development of object-centred theories within fashion studies is inevitable. However, the resultant dependency has fostered a rather one-sided perspective. After the turn of the millennium, museums held increasing numbers of stand-alone presentations of shoes. Yet these tended towards a near-exclusive emphasis on the *auteur* designer of decidedly unusual shoes, creators of the "shoe as fetish" rather than the everyday shoe of popular culture. Such museum shows have tended to focus on big-name, celebrity designers or else have showcased eccentric footwear that often drew on female gender stereotypes—echoed in exhibition names like *Shoe Obsession,*[7] *Killer Heels,*[8] or *Pleasure and Pain.*[9] Even shows with a more diverse range of exhibits, like the exhibition *Marche et démarche: Une histoire de la chaussure* at the Musée des Arts Décoratifs in Paris,[10] largely neglected mass-produced shoes. Then came a significant step forward in the field with the publication in 2017 of *Shoes: The Meaning of Style* by Elizabeth Semmelhack, senior curator of the Bata Shoe Museum in Toronto. Using the example of four basic shoe forms—sandals, boots, high heels, and sneakers—Semmelhack relates the history of shoes with a particular focus on the 20th and 21st century. Offering a wealth of illustrations and factual information, Semmelhack unpicks the objects to reveal how the meanings connoted by shoes have changed over the years, particularly with regard to gender. Although the author's primary focus is on North America and Europe, she frequently relates the subject matter to other cultures—referring, for example, to the Persian origins of the high heel.

Faced with a collection of some several thousand shoes, the interrelationship between fashion studies and material culture was of particular significance to us. As Peter McNeil has outlined, fashion studies seeks to appraise fashion-related phenomena from a transdisciplinary perspective—and so to bring together a variety of different strands, ranging from costume history (informed from a more art-historical/cultural-historical perspective), via questions relating to production aesthetics and economics, through to the critical analysis of symbolic processes and social practices.[11] Significantly, the dichotomy between costume history, which tends towards a more inductive approach, and the more deductive reasoning favoured by fashion studies, is itself an idiosyncratic feature of the research subject: while fashion is necessarily evoked through tangible objects, it is itself also an abstract concept. Fashion, then, invites a decidedly object-laden approach on the one hand and, on the other, a mode of analysis that (in extremis) foregoes objects entirely. Giorgio Riello synthesized these two approaches into the "material culture of fashion". "Material culture" is thus understood as at a point "in-between" material evidence and theoretical concept, predicated on a constant process of exchange and confrontation between the two poles:

> Material culture is not the object itself [...], but neither is it a theoretical form [...]. Material culture is instead about the modalities and dynamics through which objects take on meaning (and one of these is that of fashion) in human lives.[12]

Insights into *Bally's* History

The company was founded by Carl Franz Bally in 1851. The manufacture of shoes was based on the division of labour from the very outset, although the factory originally operated without electricity or machines. The most crucial developments in the first few decades related to the company's efforts to supply the factory with electricity and specialized machinery (which was initially imported from the United States). First served by hydropower then steam power, the factory was eventually electrified towards the end of the 19th century. The company's first *Singer* shaft sewing machine entered service in 1854, followed in 1868 by the *McKay* stitcher—marking a milestone in increased productivity.[13]

After a difficult first few years, *Bally* eventually succeeded in establishing thriving sales offices—firstly in Latin America (Montevideo in 1870, Buenos Aires in 1873), then in Europe (Paris in 1879, and finally London in 1882). As the company grew, so too did the need to open new production facilities. A decentralized approach was taken to setting up new factories, which were opened both in Schönenwerd's immediate vicinity and further afield. This made it possible for the company to employ members of rural communities, who could continue farming in parallel to their employment at *Bally*. Piecework by women working from home was also an important component of the production process. *Bally's* founder was a paternal capitalist typical of his day: in addition to providing health insurance and housing for his employees, he also created the *Bally* Park (an attraction that still warrants a visit today). On the other hand, he also vetoed such measures as the establishment of a trade union.[14]

Bally became a stock company in 1908, before being turned into a holding company in 1921. In the period covered by this study, it was the third generation—Iwan, Ernst, and Max Bally—who were at the company's helm.

The 1930s was a decade forged by the effects of the Wall Street Crash of 1929 and the ensuing wave of economic protectionism. The outbreak of the Second World War led to problems in sourcing materials and production bottlenecks. Hostilities made it impossible (or certainly much more difficult) to import and export goods; entire markets effectively disappeared. *Bally's* fortunes were once again on an upward trajectory in the postwar period, and the company was able to celebrate its centenary in 1951 in suitably lavish style. Individual portraits of the entire workforce were commissioned for the occasion—an impressive testament not only to documentary photography, but also *Bally's* appreciation of its employees. In addition to the shoe factories in Switzerland, the *Bally* holding company was by this point the owner of production plants in France, South Africa, Great Britain, Austria, and the United States. This was in addition to a number of tanneries in South America, as well as a portfolio of real estate and sales companies. Particularly important roles were played by the retail organization Arola AG (founded in 1926) and the company's advertising department (branded Agor AG, founded in 1932). During this period, *Bally* employed around 15,000 factory workers and other employees in Switzerland and abroad, with the company manufacturing some 28,000 pairs of shoes every day.

Bally made considerable efforts to achieving self-sufficiency. In addition to operating its own rubber factory and manufacturing the wooden lasts used in shoe production, the company even grew its own vegetables for the staff canteen. Founded in 1911 as the chemical-technical department, and known from 1927 as the "Experimental Institute", *Bally's* research department worked to create synthetic fabrics and glues, as well as developing new products (including a range of shoe-care products). The research department also honed sophisticated product test procedures, creating machines for quality control purposes that themselves became highly sought-after across the globe.

However, the fourth generation of the Bally family were unable to agree on the company's future direction. Like many other businesses, *Bally* struggled with the effects of globalization in the 1970s. The speculator Werner K. Rey became *Bally's* majority shareholder in 1977, before selling the company just nine months later to the arms manufacturer Oerlikon Bührle. The new owners initially kept *Bally's* business operations essentially unchanged. However, the fall of the Berlin Wall in 1989 and the end of the Cold War led to a decline in defence contracts and so the new owners fell into financial difficulties. The company's response was to sell a number of significant real-estate holdings, including the flagship store Capitol on Bahnhofstrasse in Zürich and its exclusive shop on the rue de la Madeleine in Paris. *Bally* was eventually sold to the US investment company, Texas Pacific Group. With the exception of the *Bally* Museum and Historical Archives, the site at Schönenwerd was closed down completely in 2000. The company headquarters were relocated to Caslano (in the canton of Ticino). Shoes continued to be manufactured at the new factory, as well as at facilities in Italy and outside Europe. Most recently, *Bally* was sold in 2008 to the Vienna-based Labelux group.

Contributions

From the perspective of economic history, Roman Wild unpacks the significance of the growth in sales of the fashion shoe and the controversies surrounding shoe fashion. Various parties—campaigners from the women's movement, representatives of the shoe industry, hygienists, social scientists, and politicians—had an equal role to play in the debate surrounding fashion in the interwar period. Wild's article illustrates how a very broad array of concerns, fears, and areas of expertise were invoked in contemporary discussions about fashion.

A number of the articles explore the "fashionization" of shoes, including associated discourses and the influence they brought to bear on design. Anna-Brigitte Schlittler firstly examines the increasing differentiation of shoe design during the Second World War, and the reaction of the Swiss press to these developments. One of the most striking forms to gain popularity in this period was the platform shoe, whose unusual design provoked something of a sensation. This was particularly evident in the pages of the satirical magazine *Nebelspalter:* in dozens of cartoons, the shoe functioned as a cypher for a fashion discourse in which the emergent signs of looming socio-political conflicts were first becoming apparent. In her second article, Schlittler also describes the shift from the (individual) *modelleur* to the (collective) design team. Drawing on numerous and highly diverse sources, the study sets forth a detailed picture of the industrial design process. One remarkable aspect of this period was the paradigm shift set in motion during the 1930s: *Bally* moved from a practical, technical design approach, centred around the *modelleur*—typically a trained shoemaker with creative flair—through to an organizational form that could be termed "fashion design".

Meanwhile, in a study that compares 1930s evening shoes from the *Bally* archives with shoe fashions featured in contemporary issues of US *Vogue,* Katharina Tietze reveals parallels that underline the international importance of the Swiss shoe manufacturer. The article also looks at the diverse methods employed by fashion magazines to display shoes, and examines the ways in which shoe fashion changed—with footwear that exposed the foot, for example, or featured new kinds of heel. In the following article, Daniel Späti focuses on the evolution of the types of footwear classed as "utility shoes". Besides the shoe reform propagated by doctors and hygienists, the increasing differentiation of design was driven primarily by the general transformation in shoe usage. Beyond providing protection for the foot, there was an increasing emphasis on fashion-related functions—relating, for example, to shoes' social, emotional, and symbolic facets—which in turn looped back and even influenced the design of utility shoes.

The period examined in this study not only witnessed a proliferation of innovative shoe forms, but also new materials. In her second essay "Real Gold?", Tietze adopts a historical perspective to explore this theme via the example of gold leather. In the 1930s, gold-leather evening shoes were a must-have accessory for elegant women. These luxurious shoes numbered among the *Bally* company's most exclusive products, both in terms of their design and production technology. Using X-ray microanalysis, it was possible to prove that during the period covered by this study, *Bally* had used leather indeed coated with real gold. The essay also examines the significance of gold as a colour in the fashions of a decade dominated by the fallout from the Wall Street Crash of 1929.

While *Bally* attached great importance to creating fashionable, high-quality footwear, the company also put considerable effort into developing a diverse range of methods for displaying their products and sophisticated techniques with which to market them. In "A Fairy-Tale Affair…!", Katharina Tietze describes how *Bally* shoes were displayed at the Swiss National Exposition of 1939 in Zürich. Visitors to the Fashion Pavilion there could see *Bally* products displayed in the Exports Room. In a display inspired by jewellery showcases, *Bally* shoes were presented in indirectly illuminated glass cases, which were fitted onto the wall of a mirrored gallery. The adjoining "Fashion Theatre" staged live entertainment shows where the performers' footwear was supplied exclusively by *Bally*. Moreover, each of the three vaudeville acts performed in the theatre featured a song with *Bally*-themed lyrics. Karl Egender, the architect of the building, was also responsible for every detail of the interior design. And in her article, Henriette-Friederike Herm explores the particular role assumed by the store display window, which came to function as a new arena of communication between salesperson and shopper. The *Bally* Historical Archives' wealth of visual and photographic material provides an insight into the company's extensive engagement with the medium of display window design, which was originally the remit of Arola

AG (the company's retail organization) and Agor AG (another subsidiary owned by the *Bally* holding company).

Production Matters

For a systematic history of industrial fashion, it is important to examine the entire production cycle, from manufacture and distribution through to the point of consumption.[15] Angela McRobbie outlines six factors in this cycle: manufacture and production, design, retail and sales, training and education, fashion magazines and the media, and, lastly, consumer practices.[16] McRobbie is critical of the way studies of consumption can lose sight of production and the (often precarious) conditions in which it is undertaken. Our research projects were by their very nature unable to provide a comprehensive description of this cycle, but rather sought to gain a more profound understanding of some specific aspects. This is in part due to the nature of the sources. For example, while there are interesting sources relating to sales, the actual *point of sale*—consumption—is a theme that could be little more than merely touched upon in the study, since *Bally's* archives only contain prototype models (rather than shoes destined for sale). Furthermore, it is clear that there is more to be learned about the interrelationship between production and working conditions—not least with regard to the present day.

The story of Rosa Burri, as recorded in the minutes of one directors' meeting, offers some insight into these working conditions:

> Burri Rosa, Sewing Department: Mr Trüb reports that the aforementioned drowned this morning in the River Aare. Mr Felber, a foreman in Plant B, Shafts, had had to reject [Burri's] work and instructed her to put the items right. The work was of terrible quality, as had been the case on a number of previous occasions. Otherwise, however, the girl was considered hardworking, although her work was of varying quality. About half an hour later, the girl left the premises. Her sister was then consulted, who immediately explained that [Burri] would be certain to have headed for the Aare. It seems that "going to the Aare" was frequently used as a threat at home. The family, which has 12 children, has fallen on hard times. One of the foremen, Mr Spiel-

mann of Obergösgen, learned from a neighbour of the family that the girl had spoken frequently in recent days of drowning herself in the Aare. Burri had made previous suicide attempts a long period of convalescence from a lung disease.
Decision: Mr Trüb and Felber will visit the parents, accompanied by the local priest and mayor, in order first to establish the family's circumstances and second to prevent the circulation of any false rumours. The board is satisfied that the foreman Felber bears no responsibility for the incident.[17]

Although it is impossible here to draw any conclusions about just how far working conditions at *Bally* were implicated in the young woman's suicide, her story does nevertheless illustrate how the production of high-value goods was linked to existential problems for female factory workers. Young girls employed as seamstresses were especially important to the company. *Bally* recruited workers through a strategy of decentralized factories, which made it possible to employ young women from surrounding villages. The women could thus go on living with their families, who were able to continue working in the agricultural sector. In 1901, 34.2 percent of *Bally's* workforce were under eighteen years of age. The young women usually remained in employment until marriage or the birth of their first child. Former employees would periodically take on piecework, which they could then work on at home.[18]

Fashion design continues to form an integral part of the general history and theory of design. For design lecturers such as ourselves, fashion history and design history are one and the same: just like other products, clothing—which has been designed, produced, and marketed as a mass product since the 19th century—forms part of the history of industrial design and industrialization. *Bally* is in a preeminent position to tell this story, since the company passed through every phase of industrialization in near-textbook fashion.

Our sincere thanks to *Bally*, particularly Rebekka Gerber and Ursula Gut, who are entrusted with the care of the historical artefacts in the company's Historical Archives and were always at hand to provide advice and practical assistance; to the Ballyana family foundation, which since its founding in 2000 has made a significant contribution to researching the history of *Bally* shoes; to Sigrid Schade and Sigrid Adorf, heads of the ZHdK's Institute for Cultural Studies in the Arts, for their support in the initial development of the research project; to Roman Wild for the interesting exchange of ideas; to Maja Siebrecht for her meticulous graphic design; to Marco Iori for his attentive proofreading; to Lance Anderson and his team for their expert translation; and, last but certainly not least, to the Swiss National Science Foundation for making the entire project possible.

1 For the 18th-century beginnings of the division of labour in shoe manufacturing, see Riello 2006.

2 Anna-Brigitte Schlittler (project manager), Katharina Tietze (co-manager), Daniel Späti, Roman Wild.

3 Anna-Brigitte Schlittler (project manager), Katharina Tietze (co-manager), Henriette Friederike Herm.

4 Bally—Swiss Shoes Since 1851 at the Museum für Gestaltung Zürich, 14 March to 11 August 2019; curator: Karin Gimmi; exhibition designer: Alain Rappaport.

5 See Black et al. 2013.

6 Benstock/Ferris 2001; Riello/McNeil 2005; Sudrow 2010; Riello/McNeil 2006; Semmelhack 2008; Semmelhack 2009; Nahshon, Edna: Jews and Shoes, Oxford 2008; Sudrow 2010.

7 Fashion Institute of Technology, New York, 8 February to 13 April 2013.

8 Brooklyn Museum, New York, 10 September 2014 to 1 March 2015.

9 Victoria & Albert Museum, London, 13 June 2015 to 31 January 2016.

10 Musée des Arts Décoratifs, Paris, 7 November 2019 to 22 March 2020.

11 McNeil 2010.

12 Riello, Giorgio: "The Object of Fashion: Methodological Approaches to the History of Fashion" in: Journal of Aesthetics and Culture, vol. 3, 2011. http://www.aestheticsandculture.net/index.php/jac/rt/printerFriendly/8865/12789 (accessed 18 March 2016).

13 Hundert Jahre Bally-Schuhe, 1951, p. 28.

14 Heim 2000, pp. 61–81.

15 Gaugele 2016.

16 McRobbie 1999, p. 216.

17 Board Minutes, 21 July 1938.

18 Baumann Püntener 1996.

Business Cycles in the Fashion-Shoe Industry and the Controversies Surrounding Footwear Fashion in Switzerland (1920–1940)[1]

Roman Wild

In autumn 1939, several thousand Swiss cinemagoers found themselves watching a cartoon commercial entitled *Frau Mode spielt auf!* (Lady Fashion Performs!).[2] On the screen, a woman in a red gown and a gold crown sat playing an organ [FIG. I]. It was the eponymous and all-powerful Lady Fashion, busy creating fashions for clothes, shoes, and jewellery and setting the cycles in which they should come and go. Her harmonious melodies were commands, obeyed by a stream of putti who emerged from the organ pipes and began fitting out shops. Shop-window dummies in fashionable clothes and shoes sprang to life and began to bustle about. All the way down the value chain of the shoe industry, business began to boom.

But suddenly the organ-playing stopped; Lady Fashion pressed the keys in vain. Her hard-working putti flew to the rescue at once, but before the organ could be fixed, the damage was done. A clumsy boot, wholly inappropriate for Lady Fashion's

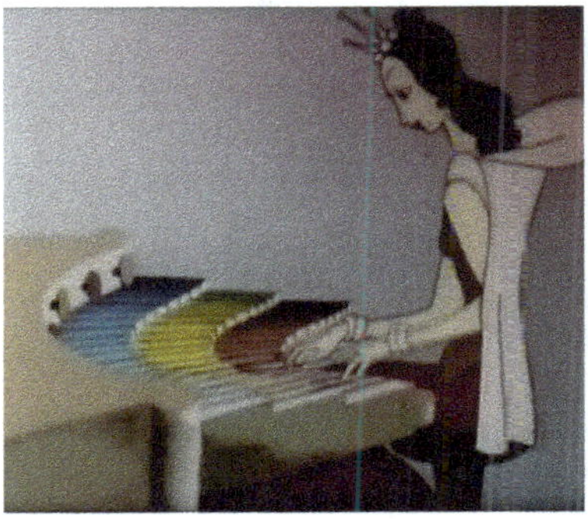

[I, II] Film stills from "Frau Mode spielt auf!", Bern 1939

sophisticated clientele, had escaped from the organ pipes [FIG. II]. On catching sight of it, the shop-window dummies fainted, and busy shoppers shrank back. It took tremendous efforts on the part of all concerned to get things running smoothly again.

After three-and-a-half minutes, this fanciful and symbolic commercial took on a concrete dimension. The cartoon figures, modelled on those of popular Walt Disney films,[3] vanished from the screen; in their place, shoes appeared. Every type of footwear was represented—sensible walking shoes, bar shoes, elegant evening shoes, high-heeled sandals [FIG. III]—manufactured in every kind of material typically available at the time. Alongside appeared the words "C.F. Bally", initially as a simple illuminated inscription, but later transforming into an animated logo. What the cinema audience was getting to see, as they waited for the main feature to roll, was *Bally's* autumn collection. The large shoe manufacturer, with outlets all over the world, had its headquarters in the Swiss town of Schönenwerd. And its autumn collection, of course, was certain to find favour with Lady Fashion.

This ad deserves a closer look for the way it reflects how the medium of film-making entered everyday life.[4] Innovative companies had been cooperating with advertisers, film-makers, and cinema owners since the early 1930s.[5] Thanks to their rich symbolism, deeply rooted in the collective memory, shoes were

[III] Production still from "Frau Mode spielt auf!", Bern 1939

ideally suited to an advertising narrative. Much more inviting for analysis are two messages which the cartoon implicitly conveys, and which, as it turns out, could not have been more controversial:

- There is no rational way of explaining what drives "the creation of fashion, a phenomenon which affects every area of our lives".[6] From its obvious psychological and social effects, however, fashion may be likened to a metaphysical force.
- This force coordinates the fluctuation of supply and demand in the clothing market. The economic up- and downswings experienced by manufacturers in the fashion industry depend on how successfully the designers of fashion items are able to anticipate the material, social, and timing criteria which drive fashion itself.

My historical analysis begins with these advertising messages. The social and economic circumstances which gave rise to *Bally's* commercial, and within which its messages resonated, form the focus of this chapter. Specifically, I am interested in the economics of fashion footwear and the controversies which surrounded it. Did the fashion sector play a significant part in the shoe consumption of the interwar period? What was the attitude of the Swiss public to the controversial and sometimes paradoxical advertising messages? How did these economic cycles and controversies relate to one another? This chapter owes many valuable ideas to the transdisciplinary and currently very popular field of material culture studies. There is no room here for a critical discussion of its premises and conclusions; however, one of the central ideas of its theory and methodology is relevant here: fashion shoes, as "everyday objects",[7] should offer a way of approaching complex human-object relationships and, as "cultural emissaries", provide "information about the state of culture and society".[8]

I address the questions posed above in two stages. First, I trace consumer demand for fashion shoes. As quantitative evidence is always plagued by gaps and simplifications, I discuss instead compelling qualitative indicators and watershed moments. As fruitful sources of data and interpretation I draw, on the one hand, on statisticians with an interest in the history of consumerism, and on the other, on the directors of *C.F. Bally AG.* Secondly, I follow the unfolding public discourse surrounding fashion shoes. Having assembled material from various sources, I examine it to uncover underlying attitudes. Of particular interest here are pressure groups and social scientists, both of whom became increasingly successful in shaping the social discourse of the 20th century.

Fashion Shoes as Everyday Consumer Goods

Whether or not shoes received the attention of leading haute-couturiers, fashion designers, commentators, and fashion-conscious consumers depended on the fashion silhouette. The First World War brought about sweeping innovations in the history of fashion that underlie all my observations in this essay.[9] These innovations required every woman who wished to be considered *à la mode* to eliminate her curves, aided by suitable undergarments, and assume a boyishly flat silhouette—a look which was intended to signify her active involvement in professional and leisure activities. The dress style favoured by women known in France as *femmes garçonnes* and in the English-speaking world as *flappers* was severely cut and usually devoid of any textile ornamentation. Because dress hems now fell to somewhere between the ankle and the knee, the feet and legs had to be (re)integrated into the body image. Thus, the shoe became an inherent part of the negotiation of what constituted "fashion". For producers, retailers, and consumers, one of the key criteria in buying and selling shoes became whether or not they were "fashionable".

This new silhouette spread from the traditional fashion capitals of Paris and London and quickly took hold in the neighbouring European countries, including Switzerland. The turning point in dress codes represented by the First World War was grasped particularly early and accurately by Elsa Gasser.[10] With a doctorate in economics, Gasser made her living as a journalist and statistician before becoming adviser to Gottlieb Duttweiler, the founder and director of the Migros supermarket chain. For the Department of Statistics of the City of Zürich, Gasser traced expenditure on clothing in the city and published her longitudinal study under the title *Zürcher Index der Bekleidungskosten* (Zürich Cost of Clothing Index) in 1924.[11] Because of the heterogeneity of the 200 officially defined ranges of clothing quality and price, producing the required survey proved to be tremendously complex. Even today, opinions are divided in the discipline of fashion studies concerning the plethora of preconditions that must be met before any quantification can be attempted and the knowledge potential which such attempts may hold. It is clear that the fashion sector cannot be summed up by a single indicator.[12] Gasser's reports are valuable because they combine the quantitative data collected (household bills from working families and price notations from manufacturing, wholesale, and retail companies) with qualitative interpretations derived from interviews (Zürich Association of Textile Retailers and other selected sources). From the quantitative perspective, Gasser stressed "differences in the price trend", citing fashion as their most important driver: "Fashion has really revolutionized the cost of a lady's dress—and by that I mean the cost of a single lady's dress made for the mass market."[13] Describing in more detail the change in the overall appearance of a lady's clothing, she wrote: "There is a far more pressing demand than before for a pleasing, modern design, both in clothes and, to a quite striking extent, in footwear."[14] According to her surveys, the altered pattern of demand "stimulated, in particular, the consumption of cheaply manufactured goods".[15]

For our purposes, the most relevant indications of shoe consumption in the 1930s come from the publications of the Pricing Commission (Preisbildungskommission). Founded in 1926, the remit of this "non-political, scientific commission, working away behind the scenes" was to process "figures and factual material" relating to everyday goods and sectors which were important to the national economy.[16] Thanks to its mandate from the Swiss Federal Council, the Pricing Commission had access to the budgets, inventories, and balance sheets of every market operator. In 1946 it presented an investigation into the shoe trade, in which, amongst other things, it arrived at the conclusion that "at least in the 12 years from 1928 to 1939, there has undoubtedly been a considerable expansion in consumption from approx. 8 to over 10 million pairs (excluding rubber overshoes)".[17] In Switzerland, two pairs of shoes were purchased per head per year. With regard to gender-specific similarities and contradictions, the Pricing Commission detected two patterns: while expenditure on men's shoes exceeded that of women in working-class families, the exact opposite was true in the case of clerical workers and civil servants: expenditure by women turned out to be almost 20 percent higher.[18] Moreover, in all social classes, women preferred to buy brand-new shoes while men preferred to repair old ones.[19] As for shoe prices, the Commission produced evidence that prices for the statistically defined "average shoe" had fallen consistently, apart from the 1927/28 season, and in the year 1935/36 had actually dropped to the prewar level.[20] Besides the development of new, i.e., more fashionable types of shoe, the reasons cited by the expert committee were the development of cheaper alternative materials, and rationalization and crises in the Swiss economy.

By now it can be established that throughout the whole of the interwar period, there was a significantly increased demand from women for "fashionable" shoes. Not even the global economic crisis, which brought with it salary reductions, part-time work, and redundancies for hundreds of thousands of consumers, could dampen this consumer demand. However, fashion shoes should not be analyzed only from the point of view of consumption; it is crucial to take into account the spheres of production and distribution and to put consumption into this context. *C.F. Bally AG* provides an ideal example for doing this. Founded in 1851 as a small manufacturing firm, it grew to become a large corporation, thanks to systematic mechanization and rationalization. Even though no one has yet written a company history of the foremost company in the Swiss shoe industry which is sufficiently detailed for the purposes of research,[21] *Bally* can nevertheless be identified as a pioneering "trailblazer"[22] in early 1920s business.

During the First World War, *Bally* had seen an enormous leap in sales and profits. When the uncertain years of the transition economy in the immediate postwar period began, the parent company in Switzerland oversaw 21 retail and 4 wholesale companies, and a further 8 subsidiaries distributed across Europe, America, and Africa. With a view to achieving optimum coordination between its many different subsidiaries, from its tannery to its wholesalers, *Bally* decided in the summer of 1921 to undergo corporate restructuring. A centrally managed holding company was founded, with its head office in Zürich.[23] "1922 will probably be the most important year for the *Bally* companies," remarked co-owner and company boss of many years, Eduard Bally-Prior,[24] as he looked forward, with just caution, to the impending readjustment of internal material, product, and finance streams.

To a not inconsiderable extent, fashion was a contributing factor in this restructuring. If *Bally* wanted to sell its shoes in foreign markets, universally protected by prohibitively high tariffs, fashion was the area on which to concentrate its efforts.[25] And if *Bally* wanted to channel its surplus capacity into the highly competitive domestic market, fashion shoes were the only answer. A report from the financial year 1934/35 puts the company strategy in a nutshell: "Today our collection is already much more fashionable than it was before. We are being more daring, and we must be more daring still if we want to improve sales."[26] The considerable managerial efforts needed to align mass production with the demands of footwear fashion are worthy of a study of their own. Two innovations which had a direct effect on the company structure must suffice here. In 1926, *Bally* took the daring decision to enter the retail market. Either by acquiring retail outlets or by buying shares in them, *Bally* took over responsibility for its own sales consultancy and retail operations. Arola was the name of this capital-intensive subsidiary, which built up a network of 72 stores in the space of 10 years, some of them situated in prime sites. From the point of view of those responsible at *Bally*, having their own retail operation meant having a channel "through which to trial fashions and fashion trends before rolling them out to the world of shoes".[27] In 1934 Agor was founded; its purpose, according to its articles of incorporation, to extract the "maximum value from our monopoly status in the fashion world".[28] Agor built up a media alliance to advertise new shoe creations with the help of famous graphic artists, photographers, filmmakers, and architects. *Frau Mode spielt auf!* is just one example of a long series of advertising campaigns.

By way of an interim conclusion, we can say that the 1920s and 1930s represented a unique highpoint for the fashion shoe, so far as both the relative proportion and the absolute number of fashion shoes are concerned. A corresponding economic boom has been noted for the London clothing industry in the same period.[29] As can be seen from the graph below[30] [FIG. IV], there was a fashion-induced expansion in the range of shoes available; for example, in the spring season of 1935, *Bally* offered its predominantly female clientele 1175 shoe products. "Any novelty or caprice was enough to make a fashionable product out of," admitted the manager of the *Bally* corporation, Hermann Stirlin, in a moment of retrospective self-criticism.[31] A strong impetus came from customers' ever-greater demand for fashion shoes. It is important to see that *Bally* anticipated this trend and fuelled it further by its deliberate company strategy and reorganization. Analyzing the resulting consumer boom, it is impossible to say whether the producer was led by the customer or the customer by the producer.

Shoe Fashion in Everyday Discourse

What was the social response to the triumphant march of the fashion shoe? We can say right away that the discourse surrounding fashion footwear also experienced a boom. Lady Fashion, as envisioned at the beginning of this article, may have

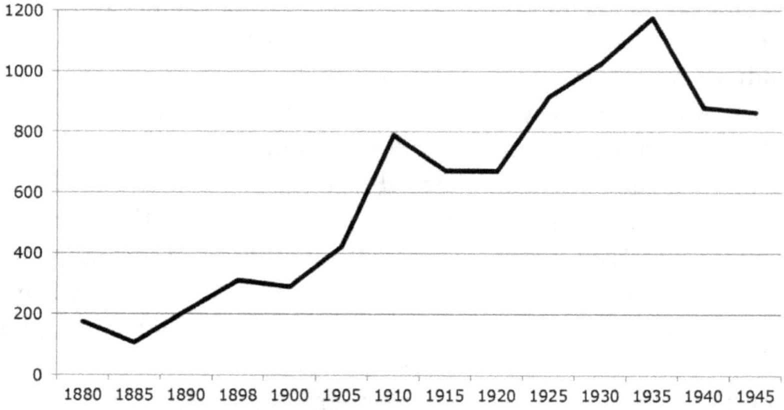

[IV] Shoe items on offer from Bally Schuhfabriken AG (spring catalogues)

been the artificial creation of a cartoon studio, but a review of hundreds of articles, brochures, and analyses from the sphere of the shoe industry shows that "Lady Fashion" was omnipresent outside the movie theatres too. The *Bally* ad played on three images so regularly invoked in the context of sartorial objects and practices as to have become everyday figures of speech.[32] While the metaphor of a "Lady Fashion" emphasized, on the one hand, the supposedly gender-specific characteristics of volatility, impulsiveness, and unpredictability, the idea of a "fashion queen" highlighted fashion's powerful, imperious, and subjugating aspects. The image of the "scourge of fashion", on the other hand, focused more on the damage, illness, and injuries for which fashion was held responsible.

The fascinating thing about metaphors of this sort is that they not only organize the way people speak but also the way they think and act. As George Lakoff and Mark Johnson have convincingly shown, they were and are used in everyday life to adapt the new and unknown, reduce fear and anxiety, express what cannot be said in ordinary discourse, and turn the future into something which can be shaped and planned.[33] In the metaphors we are discussing here, several strands of discourse converge—discourses which were circulating transnationally, and which in equal measure defined problem areas and offered solutions to them.[34] They maintained their potency, because various social players in the interwar period tried to imbue them with their own messages, in a game of repetition and modification. In what follows, without making any claim to be exhaustive, I summarize the five most prominent discursive strands surrounding fashion footwear.

1. One of the most pronounced critics of fashion shoes was the women's movement.[35] In the interwar period, empowered by its involvement in the semi-state-controlled war economy during the First World War, it articulated behavioural requirements and prohibitions for every sphere of everyday life. "What a lack of culture and style, what ephemerality and extravagance the concept of fashion implies: from shoes with high heels, from thin stockings which often hardly last a day and must be endlessly darned [...]—it is one long

chain of extravagance, impracticality, and ephemerality."[36] Fashion became a problem because it was held responsible for consumer spending on items as short-lived as they were expensive; spending, moreover, which threatened to break the hard-pressed budgets of blue-collar, white-collar, and middle-class working families. Whenever the economic outlook was bleak, the condemnation of the fashion shoe intensified. Aware that women were responsible for the entire household domain, handling expenditure on food and clothing amounting annually to as much as four billion Swiss francs,[37] the women's movement tried to curtail shoe fashion. As a national economic indicator, the fashion shoe was always more explosive when it was associated with the biodeterministic argument that women were inclined to make impulsive and irrational purchasing decisions.[38]

2. Under the banner of hygiene, experts began to study the foot and the garment that encased it for protection and support. It was not so much the material used for the sole and upper which attracted contributions to the debate, as the shape of the shoe itself. Arnold Heim, a far-travelled and widely-read Zürich scientist, may be cited here as an especially eloquent critic: "Nowadays foot complaints are enormously widespread. For the motto of modern society is 'better to suffer than to renounce fashion'. It is this motto, not hygienic considerations, which the large manufacturers pursue, for whom the only important concern is their business."[39] Heim demanded that consumers and producers restrict themselves to classic shoe designs, which respected the anatomy of the foot. In the 1930s, the way in which the shapes of shoes were changing to suit the dictates of fashion came to the attention of doctors who had dedicated themselves to the prevention of deforming and degenerative conditions.[40] Contemporary research suggested that the foot complaints caused by fashion shoes would be inherited by the next generation and could entail a heavy burden for the future economy and defence capability of the Swiss people.[41]
3. In the fashion discourse of the 1920s and 1930s, the voice of industry was very audible.[42] In the opinion of its representatives, the transformation of the shoe from a basic commod-

ity to an item of optional expenditure was worrying.[43] In this context we may quote the Schweizerischer Werkbund (Swiss Association for Art and Design), whose president, Georg Schmidt, declared in accusatory tones in a lecture in 1944: "One has only to take a walk through one of our consumer-goods factories—whether it be a shoe factory, a carpet factory, a chair factory, a lamp factory, or a porcelain factory—to see how producers are also held victim by [the scourge of] fashion!"[44] Schmidt's criticism was aimed at the curtailment of product life cycles, as well as at the practice, observable in industry, of neglecting aesthetic and material considerations in product design. In addition, trade-union representatives were afraid that "Lady Fashion" could destroy the livelihoods of shoe repairers and bespoke and orthopedic shoemakers. Severe criticism was levelled by the industry journal *Schweizerische Schuhmacher-Zeitung* at the large shoe companies: "The public has been plied with a surfeit of fashion items of the most extreme kind, and the speculation that it would always be possible to keep increasing sales of such items has backfired, and roundly at that. The result is a sales crisis, price cuts, losses, fire sales, and general price erosion."[45] One-man companies were close to ruin, it declared, and the risk exposure involved in the production, sale, and repair of fashion shoes was no longer acceptable. When the shoe industry, as a result of cut-throat competition, began to focus more strongly than ever on the fashion-shoe sector, the fashion-critical discourse reached its peak. In 1936, the magazine *Schuhhandel,* the second biggest business periodical of the Swiss shoe industry, issued a demand for a fashion commission, which would meet three or four times a year and include representatives of all the professions involved. What the initiators had in mind was an "on-going control of fashion"[46] following international models.[47]

4. The distortions of the Swiss shoe market in the 1930s called for regulation by the state authorities.[48] In the context of commissioning preparatory reports, social scientists were asked to evaluate the fashion phenomenon. It was regarded as a foregone conclusion that fashion would complicate

companies' manufacturing technology and process organization and delay the achievement of optimum economic production.[49] The scientists consulted were also aware of other controversial aspects of shoe consumption. "Like the economist, the sociologist must also express his concern that broad swathes of consumers are feeling increasingly dissatisfied with the artificial creation of fashions in the realm of footwear, because their income does not allow them to keep up with every stage of the manufacturers' race to bring out the latest models."[50] It was thought that fashion items had the potential to cause disturbance, sufficient, in the case of Switzerland—a "classless society"—to lead to social conflict. At this point, the discipline of applied psychology entered the debate, in the person of Franziska Baumgarten-Tramer.[51] The private lecturer teaching at the University of Bern believed that mass psychological damage was being suffered by women as a result of commercially motivated changes of fashion. In 1938, in the periodical *Gesundheit und Wohlfahrt*, she published the following diagnosis: "It is, thus, a matter of a failure of knowledge, capability, and will."[52] Many women, she held, did not know which clothes and shoes were in fashion, so that they were unable to make a choice; many women did not have the financial means to keep up with the changes in fashion; and many women gave up fashion for reasons of good sense, but in return were punished by social disdain.

5. A fifth and final strand of discourse can be detected in the discussion surrounding "Lady Fashion". For Switzerland, the Second World War did not mean military action, but it did mean shortages, rising prices, and the falling quality of everyday items. To prevent the sort of shortages which had occurred towards the end of the First World War,[53] state rationing programmes and statutory economic measures were introduced.[54] Because it was not known how long the war would last, the mood was tense: a shortage of materials was not compatible with product variety. In particular, trade unionists and social-democratic activists protested about unequal consumer opportunity and irresponsibly invested production resources.[55] This discontent crystallized around

the concept of luxury. The pros and cons were even debated by the Swiss Federal Assembly,[56] where National Council member Adolf Gloor brought the following motion in 1942: "Is the Bundesrat [Federal Council] prepared to enact the necessary legislation to ensure that the available raw material is not used for fashion articles?"[57] During the Second World War, fashion shoes came to exemplify waste, decadence, and what could be done without.

How is this indefatigable discourse about "Lady Fashion" to be explained? One of the themes exhaustively examined by material culture studies is the polyvalence of everyday items, which allows them to be perceived and interpreted in many different ways, depending on the context. Obviously, the more fundamentally the speakers disagree, the further apart these interpretations become. Nevertheless, it is striking that the interventions by social scientists were so numerous and so critical. There are plausible reasons for this level of engagement:

- Firstly, we may note a secular trend towards the "scientification of society".[58] During the 19th century, and to an even greater extent in the 20th century, businesses, officials, and parliaments increasingly called on representatives of the social sciences to explain and manage areas of conflict. The rational analysis of seemingly irrational social phenomena, like footwear fashion, was a challenge which such scholars and scientists willingly took up. While the first systematic attempts at theorization can be dated to the end of the 18th century, the second half of the 19th century saw theoretical contributions of lasting value being made by representatives of psychology, sociology, and economics.[59]
- Secondly, these academics should be taken seriously as concerned members of society. Everyday items and sartorial practices offered the ideal opportunity to popularize established knowledge and concepts. Gabriele Mentges argues that fashion very frequently had the "function of mediator and patron of new knowledge".[60] Such fashion-specific interventions were presumably made, though, not only with the intention of enlightening society, but also in the

service of state control. Raising the problem of footwear fashion seemed to academics a good way of demonstrating the socio-political usefulness of their own disciplines and acquiring financial resources for them. Fashion had arrived as a subject of everyday discourse.

- Thirdly, *C.F. Bally AG* saw and presented itself in its many commemorative publications and exhibitions as a "modern" company, receptive to scientific knowledge from whatever source. Ivan Bally, the driving force behind the company and the man who bore all the political exposure, was a promoter of "scientific management".[61] His example was emulated by other leading executives, who saw themselves as working at the interface of industry and science. By engaging in knowledge-exchange groups and conferences and contributing to publication series, *Bally* representatives entered into dialogue with many of the social scientists mentioned above and discussed the correct, scientific way of dealing with "Lady Fashion"—whether it was the director of Agor reflecting on a call for photographers for a fashion campaign,[62] the manager of the sales department explaining to an exclusive group of textile entrepreneurs the organizational principles for dealing with the "problems of fashion for business",[63] or Ivan Bally himself attempting to refute the nature-versus-culture conflict between foot and shoe, complained of by Arnold Heim.[64]

All in all, it appears that those responsible at *Bally* understood very well how embedded in the national economy their economic activities were. As director Fritz Streuli put it:

> The shoe, as a social product, is thus subject to the watchful criticism of the consumer. Rather like bread and milk, its specifications and prices are keenly followed by the public. This ensures that, for two quite different reasons, one aesthetic and the other social, there is a limit to how much we can achieve.[65]

The booms in fashion-shoe consumption and the controversies surrounding footwear fashion were thus closely interlinked. One could not be had without the other.

1 This essay is based on the PhD thesis by Wild, Roman: Auf Schritt und Tritt. Der schweizerische Schuhmarkt 1918–1948; Zürich 2019.

2 Production of Frau Mode spielt auf! was entrusted to the Pinschewer film studio. The commercial cost just short of 22,000 Swiss francs and took up around five percent of Bally's approved advertising budget. The film was shown in 58 cinemas in German-speaking Switzerland. It did not reach screens in the Suisse Romande (French-speaking cantons) until 1940. See the Historical Archives of Bally Schuhfabriken AG, Agor AG Zürich, Annual Report and Accounts 1939; Amsler 1997.

3 Tomkowiak 2008.

4 See Kurtzig 1926; Schlaepfer 1943.

5 See Bochsler/Derungs 1998.

6 Zimmermann 1943.

7 See König 2005.

8 König/Papierz 2012, p. 284.

9 Amongst the extensive literature deserving of special mention: Mundt 1989; Specker 2000.

10 See Bochsler 2014.

11 Gasser 1924.

12 It is impossible to detect a fashion factor from price series, influenced by price rises, currency fluctuations, and market trends. The amount of work needed to construct auxiliary indices can scarcely be justified. Occasionally, economists even subsume fashions as a residual value. Answers to the question, raised mostly by economists, "Fashion: Why People Like It and Theorists Do Not" can be found on the one hand in the unschooled perspective of researchers in sartorial matters and on the other in the limited modelability of the pattern of consumption. See Andreozzi/Bianchi 2007; Honeyman/Godley 2003; Polese/Blaszczyk 2012.

13 Gasser 1924, p. 124.

14 Ibid., p. 129.

15 Ibid., p. 125.

16 Kaufmann 1952.

17 Pricing Commission 1946, p. 31.

18 Ibid., p. 31.

19 Ibid., p. 32.

20 Ibid., p. 33.

21 For contemporary studies, cf. Büchi 1930; Schmid 1939; Bally Schuhfabriken AG 1951; Wild 2019.

22 Plumpe 2014, p. 18.

23 Toggweiler 1926.

24 Historical Archives of Bally Schuhfabriken AG, Eduard Bally: "Bd. 1: Geschichte C.F. Bally AG; Bd. 2: Statistische Tabellen"; Schönenwerd 1921, esp. vol. 1, p. 1645 (on CD-ROM).

25 Kamber 1933.

26 Historical Archives of Bally Schuhfabriken AG, report from Arola to the board of directors about the financial year 1934/35.

27 Bally Arola Service 1946.

28 Historical Archives of Bally Schuhfabriken AG, Agor AG Zürich, Annual Report and Accounts 1935.

29 Godley/Kershen/Schapiro 2003.

30 Historical Archives of Bally Schuhfabriken AG, sales catalogues 1880–1950; my own collection of data.

31 Stirlin 1943, p. 78.

32 Outside the shoe industry, common figures of speech concerning fashion are listed in Dingel 2006; Wild 2010; Tramer 2014.

33 Lakoff/Johnson 1998.

34 See Landwehr 2009; ibid. 2010.

35 See Stämpfli 2002.

36 David 1921, p. 102.

37 See Staudinger 1929, p. 37.

38 See Wolff 1912.

39 Heim 1942, p. 265. Heim also drew attention to his fears of degeneration through several series of articles, ibid. 1941; ibid. 28.9.1956.

40 See Thomann 1992; Linder/Saltzman 1998; Breyer 2011.

41 Author unknown 1942.

42 See Angst 1992.

43 Gnägi/Nicolai/Wohlwend 2013.

44 Schmidt/von Grüningen/Mussard 1944, p. 20.

45 Author unknown 1931.

46 Author unknown 1936.

47 On international fashion institutes and fashion commissions see Sudrow 2010, pp. 153–166.

48 See Wild 2016.

49 Kaufmann 1944, p. 32.

50 Pricing Commission 1946, pp. 85f.

51 For her career and publications, see Daub 1996.

52 Baumgarten-Tramer 1938, p. 638.

53 Wild 2013.

54 Author unknown 1941.

55 Droux 2004.

56 See Duttweiler 1942.

57 Author unknown 1942.

58 A pioneering work is Raphael 1996.

59 Mentges 2015, pp. 31–39.

60 Ibid., p. 36.

61 Jaun 1986, pp. 108–123, 202–253.

62 Klinger 1942.

63 Streuli 1944.

64 History of Science Collections of the ETH Library, HS 494: 293: Arnold Heim (1882–1965), Geologe, Forschungsreisender; Manuskripte, Fotografien, Dias, Separatsammlung aus dem Nachlass; Material zum Aufsatz "Schuhe oder Füße? Ein Mahnruf".

65 Streuli 1944, p. 15.

"Bally Shoes Are Trend-Setting Fashion Creations"[1]

Shoe Design in the Second World War

Anna-Brigitte Schlittler

The transformation of the simple utility shoe into a stylish fashion accessory is clear from even a cursory glance of the *Bally* archives. Starting in the 1930s, there was a dramatic increase in both the quantity and variety of prototypes. Rather than coming to a halt, this diversity indeed continued during the period of the Second World War. There was an extraordinary range of designs: casual shoes, heeled sandals, mountaineering boots, pumps, including of the stilettoed variety (whether for afternoon, summer, or early summer wear), "fantasy high heels", semi-sports shoes, golf shoes, models with names like *Lifties, Louis XV, Richelieus,* and *Ghillies,* school shoes, running and cycling shoes, slippers, *bottillons,* and après-ski shoes. In total, the archives contain over 400 models for women's shoes, another 160 for men, as well as children's shoes, and a wide array of designs for work and sportswear. The models stand out for their meticulous craftsmanship and sophisticated design—less apparent, however, is that such good design was very often a response to political and economic events.

Magazines are one of the most important sources for learning about a society's relationship to fashion. My focus in this essay will be on a selection of Swiss print media, since the Second World War had forced the country's shoe industry into a growing reliance on the domestic market. Switzerland experienced a dramatic collapse in exports—from a total value of 17.1 million Swiss francs in the first year of the war to an absolute low of 3.1 million francs in 1944.[2] This essay's primary focus will be on weekly illustrated magazines and daily newspapers. Magazines regularly reported on developments in the fashion world, although the theme featured less frequently in newspapers.

However, *Bally* preferred to advertise in newspapers during this period, believing that its audience would increase as more and more people sought to keep abreast of the latest war developments.[3] The satirical magazine *Nebelspalter* also accorded fashion a prominent place on its pages. In-house company publications, particularly the *Arola Hauszeitung*, represent a hitherto largely untapped historical source. Published by Arola Schuh AG (founded in 1926 as the sales division of the *Bally* holding company), the magazine appeared three times a year from 1931. Written for a trade rather than general readership, the magazine provides an insight into a part of the company notable for its almost unreservedly positive attitude towards fashion, even—indeed, particularly—during the Second World War. This pro-fashion outlook was accompanied by a note of ambivalence. While the company was beholden to Switzerland's "spiritual national defence" *(Geistige Landesverteidigung*—a cultural movement that sought to protect Swiss values and customs), it still maintained an economic interest in open global markets and a commitment to a globally interconnected fashion culture.

Raw Materials and Ersatz Materials

Dependent on imports—a maximum of 400,000 hides were produced in Switzerland annually, whereas the company needed 2 million[4]—and threatened with rationing, *Bally* was anxious from the war's outset, not merely about the general state of business but, most of all, about the procurement of the raw material of leather. Just two months into the war, Arola's managing director, M.W. Wittstock, announced the company's highest ever sales figures. However, he also bemoaned the increasing difficulty in sourcing materials and forcefully appealed to employees to make economies:

> What conclusions are to be drawn from this? We, too, must put limits on our demands, simplify our collections, and always be prepared to learn lessons from every situation. Let us not forget that there is a war on, and that in wartime the impossible can become possible. Thrift must once again be the watchword at every stage of production.[5]

The archives' collection of women's shoes is particularly illustrative of the crucial role played by design—or in-house "creation" as it was known—in putting this more economical approach to raw materials into practice, and the creativity involved in integrating new and unusual materials.

Numerous models of shoes have uppers made from woven textiles such as satin, linen (or hemp), and viscose. Alternative leathers were used to make shoes, such as crocodile, snake, and even fish leather (which required great delicacy of workmanship), often in combination with conventional leather and suede. Animal skins were also put to use, from conventional furs (such as foal, cow, and sea lion) through to more exotic varieties (leopard, ocelot, and cheetah).

A particularly successful model, and one of the few innovations to emerge from the slowed fashion cycle of the war years, was the "après-ski shoe". In December 1942, the *Neue Zürcher Zeitung* reported on the "onward victorious march of the après-ski shoe".[6] The report noted that après-ski footwear, once "suitable only for the health spa", had been worn as street fashion since the second winter of the war.[7] These shoes were typically rubber-soled, although a number of the particularly unusual models came with thick soles made of cork [FIG. 1].

[1] Après-ski shoes, 1940s
(photo: Manuel Fabritz, © Bally)

Often covered in fabric or leather, this light-weight material was also used to sole summer sandals and for wedge heels (the latter being a feature of the *Lifty* model).

From 1942, wood was another material used for making sandal soles—sole leather having been banned from the beginning of that year.[8] Heavy and inflexible—not to mention bearing the stigma of poverty—wooden shoes presented a challenge both in terms of design and production technology. As well as the *Bambino* children's shoe, *Bally* launched two models whose wooden soles each boasted a distinct design: The *Intermezzo* (featuring a hinge joint), and the *Pergola* (with a three-section sole).

Despite the fact that *Bally's* sandals were relatively comfortable to wear, exempt from rationing restrictions,[9] and came in a wide choice of materials and dyed soles, they only started "flying off the shelves" once they had managed to convince the buying public that wood was fashionable:

> A fashion made necessary by the war, admittedly, and one that also does our country a tremendous service by helping save on (the now very limited) stocks of sole leather.[10]

The highlight of the advertising campaign was a specially composed song, "Holz ist die grosse Mode"/"C'est la mode du bois" (Wood's the height of fashion).

> [O]ne thing's for certain: The whole of Switzerland talked about it, not least in response to the various attacks on our slogan. Its resonance across Switzerland is clear from the various humorous articles featured in "Nebelspalter", "Sie und Er", and several other illustrated magazines, not to mention a good number of valuable articles penned by journalists and fashion writers.[11]

In addition to wood, actual ersatz materials were also used in the manufacture of shoes. These include a product known in German as *Werkstoff* (a generic term meaning "material")—essentially, an artificial leather made from ground off-cuts of tanned leather, then mixed with cellulose and a binding agent.[12] At *Bally,* it was used mainly in the manufacture of heels.[13]

The creative approach to using valuable raw materials is immediately striking. Even the smallest leather off-cuts were used for decorative features in the form of colourful bobbles on laces, contrastingly coloured decorative seams, intricate appliqués, and playful loops and frills. Embroidery is another striking feature of the shoes. Sometimes delicate, sometimes more rustic in style, the decorations were embroidered in shiny yarn—although occasionally more "modest" materials like raffia and straw would be used [FIG. II].

Overall, this was very far from a "simplified collection" and much more a display of ambitious industrial design. To date, the evolution, structure, and working practices of the company's design department have not been studied in any great detail. It is possible to get an impression of the department's work culture from an undated (and clearly staged) photo, which shows a number of employees (including the "head of creation",[14] Max Matter) comparing shoes for quality purposes. Strips of wood are visible on the workbench, alongside a number of magazines, such as *Vogue*.

[II] Summer shoes, 1940s
(photo: Manuel Fabritz, © Bally)

"He anticipates the changes of the era and his creations maintain Bally products' excellent reputation as international fashion shoes."[15] The high esteem enjoyed by the company's *créateurs* was to a large extent down to the commercial success of their fashion shoes—between 1928 and 1939, *Bally* was able to increase annual production from 8 to 10 million pairs.[16] The pages of Switzerland's press, in both German- and French-speaking cantons, reveal the variety and range of products sold by *Bally* during the war. One advertisement from 1939 proclaimed: "Our extremely abundant collection of delightful, Bally-patented creations allows you to make the choice that suits you."[17] This was no idle boast. *Bally* advertised new products, usually available in a variety of colours, on a near-weekly basis.[18]

At the same time, the attitude towards fashion—that "great, influential tyrant"[19]—was ambiguous.[20] The transition from utility good to consumer product manufacturing entailed "the momentous phenomenon of changing fashions". [21] The design team's evident delight in the sheer variety of fashion was shared by the staff of Arola AG—save for the occasional complaint about "customers' extravagant demands".[22] Fashion was viewed unequivocally as the major selling point:

> It is essential that every effort is made to undergird the fashionability of our products. Say, for example, our product line on display in every store were to consist merely of simple, ordinary shoes, then our female customers would soon start buying fewer pairs. The aim of fashion, then, is to whet the appetite to buy more.[23]

"Heavy Heels and the Look of the Platform Sole Are the Flavour of the Day"[24]

Shoes with platform soles or wedge heels stand out for their particularly striking form. Conspicuously thick-soled shoes have been a constant in European costume history. Whether sturdy peasant clogs, *chapines* (a richly ornamented hybrid of Spanish and Arab design), or *calcagnini* (the notoriously decadent luxury product worn by the Venetian elite)—all bear material witness to the richness of design, symbolism, and cultural meaning associated with this unusual style of footwear.

In the 1930s, platform shoes[25] made their first appearance as a fashionable, industrially mass-produced item, and went on to inspire the imaginations of designers and consumers alike. As Elizabeth Semmelhack has observed, platform shoes are "potent markers of up-to-the-minute stylishness, an intentionally striking display of the wearer's active participation in fashion".[26] In the following section, this avowedly fashionable object will be viewed in the context of contemporary fashion discourse, which—as will be demonstrated—became involved in the disputes on national identity and the meaning of gender.

The innate willingness of the fashion-conscious to be open to anything new made this unfamiliar shoe both a much sought-after accessory and a target for scorn and criticism.

For the fashionable consumers of industrial mass products, the thick-soled shoes were *de rigueur.* So were they for numerous youth (sub)cultures, such as the *swing boys* and *swing girls* of Zürich, the French *Zazous*,[27] and the *Ottakringer Schlurfs* of Vienna, whose footwear became, "by means of additional old rubber soles, the coveted *Doppelbock* [double-mount]".[28] What is furthermore striking about platform shoes is their cross-gender appeal, which is all the more remarkable given the clear delineation between men's and women's footwear since the late 18th century.[29]

"The Modern Woman Wears [...] the Glass Heel with In-Built Goldfish Bowl"[30]

Swiss publications continued to report on fashion during the war. Alongside *Annabelle,* whose first issue came out in 1938, Swiss readers with an interest in fashion could turn to *L'Illustré* in (francophone) western Switzerland, and two weekly magazines—*Schweizer Illustrierte* and *Sie und Er* in the central and eastern cantons. The latter in particular featured weekly reports about the latest fashion trends, some running over several double-page spreads, while also providing fashion advice and, as the war dragged on, tips on how best to save and re-use materials. Shoes were given relatively little attention, in spite of having grown in significance as a fashion accessory (at this point in time, full-body shots were not yet the norm in Swiss fashion photography). On rare occasions, there might be full-page illustrations in which shoes featured prominently alongside bags, hats, gloves, umbrellas, and silk scarves.[31] Even rarer were reports devoted exclusively to shoes, such as the article about *Bally* published in *Annabelle* with the heading: "The blue ribbon of Swiss quality: The shoe from Schönenwerd."[32]

From 1942, reports on shoes with platform soles or wedge heels appeared more frequently; although as often as not, they raised points relating to the war economy rather than fashion—a feature on "ersatz materials", [33] for example, or a short column headlined "What will we be walking on this summer—cork, wood, or straw?"[34] One exception was a report published in *Sie und Er*. Headlined "Wood is today's big fashion"[35]—a direct allusion to one of *Bally's* advertising slogans—the article reported on a special display ("Wood in the Service of Fashion") exhibited at the sample fair in Basel.

Rather surprisingly at first, the satirical magazine *Nebelspalter* depicted *Bally* shoes—entirely consistent with the company's self-image—as advanced fashion products [FIG. III].

Die moderne Frau trägt..
BALLY
Aquarium
... den Glasabsatz mit eingebautem Goldfisch-Aquarium

[III] Bolleter, "The Modern Woman Wears [...]" (Nebelspalter no. 28, 9 Jul. 1942)

The "Goldfish Bowl" was just one of dozens of fashion-themed cartoons[36] published in *Nebelspalter* during the war years. This was in contrast to satirical magazines outside Switzerland, such as *Punch, Kladderadatsch,* or *Le Canard enchaîné,* which seldom, if ever, paid attention to fashion.

Having expanded its print-run from just a few hundred copies in the 1920s to 30,000 in 1945,[37] *Nebelspalter* enjoyed (and continues to enjoy) a reputation as an important weapon in the nation's "spiritual defence" *(Geistige Landesverteidigung),* "the integrationist ideology that propagandized the unity of nation and state, forged through an intense process of introspection on what is 'typically Swiss', and a resistance to the alien".[38] The weekly had been swift to adopt an anti-Nazi stance right from 1933. This resulted in a "mythologization of its own past",[39] beginning immediately after the war and to some extent still going on today. Little room was thus left for critical reflection

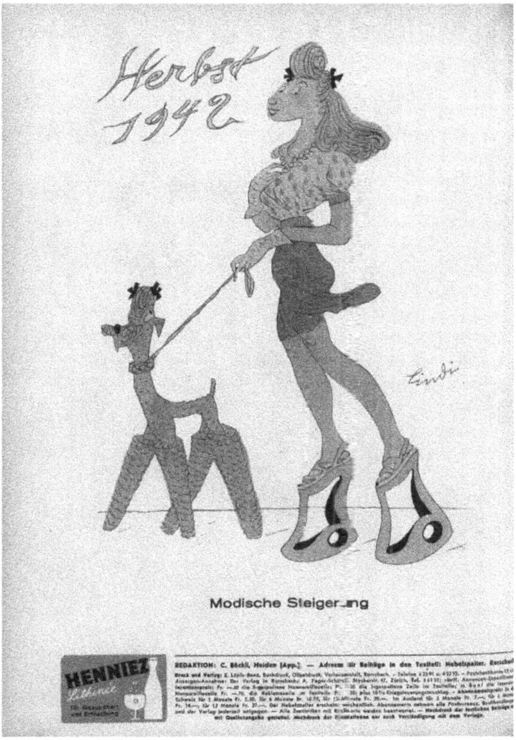

[IV] Lindi, "Autumn 1942—Stepped-up Fashion" (Nebelspalter no. 41, 1 Oct. 1942)

on its endeavour "against red and brown fists"[40] (i.e., Communist and Nazi thuggery) being not strictly progressive but tainted with anti-urban, anti-American, sexist, and racist tendencies.

The magazine's satirical gaze fell with particular regularity on contemporary shoe fashions. The prime targets for mockery were almost always shoes with platform soles and wedge heels, which attracted attention by dint of their sculptural appearance and the dramatic effect they had on the female silhouette.

Many of the drawings operate within the classic framework of fashion cartoons, typically based on creating "figures of fun". The cartoons' "primary purpose is to be funny and entertain".[41] Each new fad in the fashion world provided yet more satirical fodder [FIG. IV].

Another characteristic of the platform shoe was its ability to lend women's bodies "unnatural" height, which presumably threatened the established order of the sexes [FIG. V].

Swiss-Baby, *Züri-Schnuggerli*, and Swingling: The Cartoons of Ernst Schoenenberger

Another important frame of reference in the relationship between satire and fashion is the unusual body of work created by

[v] Merz, "In for a Penny, in for a Pound!" (Nebelspalter no. 32, 8 Aug. 1941)

[VI] Ernst Schoenenberger, "Swing Voice on the Want of FHD" (Nebelspalter no. 39, 30 Sept. 1943)

the cartoonist Ernst Schoenenberger (1911–1963). From 1942 to the end of the war, over 30 of his cartoons were published in *Nebelspalter*—more than half of which appeared on the front cover. In 1950, the magazine's publishers even released a special issue featuring 80 of his cartoons.

Pride of place in these invariably large-scale drawings was almost always given to young women dressed in the very latest fashions. The women's appearance is made all the more striking by their footwear, which Schoenenberger rendered with considerable attention to detail: He hardly ever repeated the same pair of shoes or resorted to formulaic representations. His work even included images drawn "from life", such as the shoe appliquéd with a squirrel motif [FIG. XII]—drawings of which featured in numerous Swiss magazines, having first appeared in *L'Illustré* in late December 1944.[42]

Clearly, Ernst Schoenenberger was remarkably well informed about fashion, to the extent that creations by such renowned shoe designers as Salvatore Ferragamo are easily recognizable in his drawings. The cartoonist also used clothes as a way to visually drive home his message (the female puppeteer, for instance, both manipulates and panders to men). Thus, we see that the female protagonist's blouse is a fashionable variation of

Züri-Görl
„Sie chömmich ruig uslache Sie, Ine gseht me ja vo wytem aa dassi en Chabis verschtönd vom hütige Swing!"

[VII] Ernst Schoenenberger, "Zürich Girl" (Nebelspalter no. 36, 3 Sept. 1942)

the uniform jacket worn by the "American who dropped from the sky" [FIG. XI]. Being up-to-speed on the latest fashions was far from the norm among 20th-century cartoonists. As Gundula Wolter has shown, cartoons that took a close interest in contemporary fashion had begun to fall out of favour as early as the 1830s.[43]

The cartoons employ iconography drawn primarily from US visual culture, and specifically "pin-ups"—a genre that became especially popular during the Second World War. These full-length pictures showed women in minimal (or figure-hugging) clothing, shown in poses that conveyed narrative.[44] The genre's heyday was from 1920 to 1950, when magazines faced increasing competition, and illustrators were employed with the specific remit of attracting readers.[45] The exaggerated female body forms and poses, and the pictures' narrative element can also be seen in Schoenenberger's cartoons. Many of his female characters are portrayed with a note of sexual aggression and latent hostility towards men. These traits are shared by the popular *femme fatale* figure of the era, who graced the front covers of contemporary pulp magazines and became emblematic of vi-

Dem Swingling ein kräftiges Prost Neujahr vom Kreiskommando!

[VIII] Ernst Schoenenberger, "To the Swingling, New Year's Greetings from Local Command" (Nebelspalter no. 52, 30 Dec. 1943)

Swiss-Baby am Start
„Hällo! Boys!! Ai kamm!!!"

[IX] Ernst Schoenenberger, "Swiss Baby at the Starting Blocks" (Nebelspalter, no. 32, 9 Aug. 1945)

sual culture's nascent fascination with "the bizarre". However, artists working in these popular genres invariably depicted women wearing extremely stilettoed heels, whereas Schoenenberger preferred to draw shoes with platform soles or vertiginous wedge heels. The cartoon highlights Schoenenberger's active participation in contemporary fashion-critical discourse, underscored by a rigidly dualistic view of gender that would not tolerate even the slightest deviation.

It was precisely this strict demarcation of female and male roles that was challenged by the events of the Second World War. Countless women entered civilian working life to assume roles previously occupied by men, before eventually even taking on functions in the military (Switzerland here being no exception). Whether working as carpenters, welders, or bakers, women fighting on the "domestic front" were invariably represented in a positive light in the illustrated weekly press.[46] By contrast, women's inclusion in the army caused palpable anxiety and unease. The Women's Auxiliary Service *(Frauenhilfsdienst*, or FHD) was founded in 1940. *(Bally* even responded with the creation of a specially designed shoe for servicewomen.) Roles were clearly defined: The Auxiliary Service was voluntary, and women who served were restricted to supporting functions. Although large numbers of women initially volunteered, the intake of new recruits fell dramatically from as early as 1941.[47] It did not escape army command that women's reluctance to sign up might in some way reflect frustration at being denied political rights (it was not until 1971 that Swiss women were able to vote in federal elections). Colonel Vaterlaus, who headed the Auxiliary Service from 1942, felt that it was unbecoming of women "in the present time" to make their vital contribution to the army contingent on a political *quid pro quo.*[48] Meanwhile, Schoenenberger glibly dismissed women's reluctance to volunteer as a mere matter of clothing [FIG. VI].

Bally was also prey to the widespread fear of women becoming more masculine:

> Today's woman knows that she might be conscripted to the armed forces, which is precisely why she has to dress in a way that maintains her femininity and charm. In terms of silhouette and details, she

refrains from outdated excess and eagerly follows a fashion whose soft feminine lines lend congenial expression to a quietly optimistic serenity.[49]

Anti-Americanisms

Although the cartoons derive their form from US popular culture and riff on its visual iconography, much of their content is anti-urban, anti-American, racist, and sexist.

This was rooted in cultural anti-Americanism—a rather astonishing sentiment, given Switzerland's geopolitical situation in the early 1940s. The ingredients for this attitude are already evident in some of the early cartoons from 1942. Striding energetically through the picture on very high platform shoes is a meticulously coiffured and fashionably dressed woman. This "sassy Zürich girl" cuts a striking figure: long pointed nails painted red, full mouth emphasized with blazing-red lipstick, with the look topped off with a flashy pair of sunglasses. The caption addresses readers directly, telling them they know nothing about "today's swing" [FIG. VII].

Das Trophäen-Beybi

[x] Ernst Schoenenberger, "The Trophy Baby" (Nebelspalter no. 16, 18 Apr. 1945)

While the later cartoons are more focused on current affairs, the representation of female protagonists continued to use the template of young, fashionable urban women who were characterized by their obsession with swing and US culture while brimming with sex appeal.

Zürich was indeed an important centre for jazz and swing in Switzerland. Internationally celebrated musicians performed at the *Esplanade* and *Grand Café Sihlporte.*[50] Although people spoke of these performances in favourable and even knowledgeable terms,[51] there was little understanding for either the young "swing generation" or the associated club culture. An illustrative example of this attitude can be found in an article published in 1943 in the *Neue Zürcher Zeitung*. As well as describing the young people's purportedly Americanized (body) language, the journalist writes extensively about their trademark look, singling out the "cork-soled buskins", short skirts, and red-varnished finger nails favoured by "swing girls", and the excessively long jackets and hair of the "swing boys" (accessorized with the obligatory pack of *Lucky Strikes).* The article's tone grows increasingly strident, resorting to the same tropes as Schoenenberger in calling for "post-education" and military service as a means to instill discipline into insubordinate youths:

> We are guaranteed one solace, however: Times are hard, and that is something the swing generation cannot escape. One day, they will receive their summons to basic training, aerial defence, or agricultural service. Life there will swing to a rather harsher (and entirely unmistakable) rhythm. They generally emerge from this different style of swing with clear eyes and newly steadied legs.[52] [FIG. VIII]

While *Nebelspalter* had previously adopted an anti-urban stance—or, more specifically, an anti-*Zürich* stance (Zürich being the largest city in Switzerland and therefore an alleged hotspot for vice)—the intensification of its explicit anti-Americanism, combined with racism and a firm line in the "battle of the sexes", marked a new development. In an essay entitled "Feindbild Amerika" (The American Bogeyman), Dan

Diner describes how the transformation of women's roles—a phenomenon that first emerged in the United States—became the target of virulent hostility from certain swathes of the European population in the 1920s.[53] Women came to be viewed as tyrannical authority figures who paid the price of equality through the loss of their "innate" femininity. While the figure of the "American Woman" may have been an object of desire, she did not inspire respect.[54] [FIG. IX]

As the war progressed, Schoenenberger's female characters took on an increasingly aggressive appearance and a more explicitly sexual undertone. The women he drew were desirable, yet also monstrous and sinister, with a predilection for "hunting" and "killing" men [FIG. X].

One contemporary development that may have prompted this imagery was an agreement concluded with the United States, permitting (effective from summer 1945) US officers and soldiers to take leave of duty in Switzerland.[55] Some 300,000 GIs duly travelled to Switzerland, unleashing all manner of (erotic) fantasies and fears among the Swiss population. Women soon fell under general suspicion of engaging in sexual relationships with the newly arrived war heroes,[56] to the detriment of Swiss men—an anxiety that Schoenenberger had expressed a year previously [FIG. XI].

More disturbing than relationships with GIs were those with black GIs. One police inspector in Basel remarked: "[...] in fact, the most shameful aspect of this for our country [is] that black men [are] by far and away the most favoured"[57] [FIG. XII].

It was not just contact with GIs that stirred up resentments. Published in early 1945, this cartoon marks a response to the soldiers who had been interned since mid-1940 in camps run by the Swiss army.[58] "Daisy Tüpfi" is portrayed as an exotic (even animalistic) mythical creature, while her cocky companion "Hula Wumba"—here, Schoenenberger was probably alluding to the West African *tirailleurs sénégalais* of the French army—is characterized by the sort of racial stereotypes familiar from Jim Crow and minstrel shows.

The cartoon's historic significance is all the more potent for being published just ten years after Zürich Zoo's last ever "human zoo", when visitors were invited to gawp at an enclosure of people from European colonies (including Senegal).[59] Men once observed from a safe distance were now "on the prowl" in Swiss everyday life.

Interpreted against the Grain

Belying a conservative—indeed, reactionary—message, Ernst Schoenenberger's cartoons also convey glamour and cosmopolitanism. Although fashion is presented as a by-word for shameless sensuality and unbridled consumption, Schoenenberger's scrupulously observed understanding of the latest trends and his characteristically jaunty style—coupled with an eclectic visual vocabulary—make his drawings considerably more attractive than many of the fashion illustrations published in Switzerland during this period. As a cartoonist, he had a knack for capturing the materiality and swish of fabric to great effect.

This cosmopolitan spirit was shared by *Bally*. Even during the war years, the company acknowledged fashion's international character—not just for commercial reasons, but also as a kind of trademark corporate approach. Thus, the company

[XI] Ernst Schoenenberger,
"The American Who Dropped from the Sky—Our Newest Rival"
(Nebelspalter no. 45, 21 Apr. 1944)

[XII] Ernst Schoenenberger,
"Happy End"
(Nebelspalter no. 6, 8 Feb. 1945)

regularly included extensive reports from the world's fashion capitals in its in-house publications, while voicing its appreciation of forward-thinking shoe design in the United States and Italy, and ultimately rejecting the notion of "national" fashion. Writing after the Nazi occupation of Paris, Grete Trapp, the company's fashion correspondent, observed:

> For the first time in over a century, it is impossible to get hold of the latest fashion news from Paris. [...] This has not brought fashion to a grinding halt. It has only resulted in certain delays, while people (firstly) look around for new sources of inspiration, and (secondly) use the loss of Paris as an impromptu spur to take the initiative in expanding their own skills. Significantly, the event has not resulted in a single country retreating into an isolationist approach to fashion, tinged by nationalism. Quite the opposite. [...] In fact, we wouldn't even dream of advocating such a thing as "Swiss fashion".[60]

As a number of recent publications have shown, fashion was not simply consigned to the margins in times of war. It could be viewed in a variety of ways: as a means to uphold and communicate totalitarian ideology,[61] as an important economic factor,[62] and as a way for individuals to take conscious control of their appearance and so defy the life-threatening chaos that surrounded them.[63] With Switzerland spared direct involvement in the Second World War, the country's fashion discourse anticipated some of the conflicts that characterized the postwar years, such as teenage subcultures, the blurring of gender boundaries, mass consumerism, and the influence of US popular culture.

1 "Bally-Schuhe sind tonangebende Modeschöpfungen", Annabelle 1 (1938), n.p.

2 Swiss Federal Statistical Office, http://www.bfs.admin.ch/bfs/portal/de/tools/search.html/ (accessed 29 February 2016).

3 Agor's annual company report for 1939, published 15 December 1940.

4 Update for 1942; Arola Hauszeitung, no. 32, April 1942, p. 6.

5 "Welche Schlussfolgerung ergibt sich daraus? Wir müssen ebenfalls unsere Ansprüche zurückstellen, unsere Kollektionen vereinfachen und immer bereit bleiben, die Schlussfolgerungen aus jeder Situation zu ziehen. Ver-

gessen wir nie, dass wir im Krieg sind, und dass in einem Krieg das Unmögliche möglich werden kann. Sparsamkeit auf der ganzen Linie muss wieder dominieren." Arola Hauszeitung, no. 25, September/October 1939, p. 1.

6 "Siegeslauf des Après-Skischuhs," NZZ, 13 December 1942, p. 21.

7 "[...] bloss kurortgemässe Après-Ski-Stiefel", ibid.

8 "The supply and purchase of punched-out leather soles, and the production of leather soles from makeshift cuts of leather, are forbidden" (Swiss War Economy Ordinances, no. 55, art. 2, p. 124).

9 The sale of shoes with "ration coupons" had been subject to state regulation since 1941 (Swiss War Economy Ordinances, no. 57, p. 170).

10 "Allerdings als kriegsbedingte Mode, die zugleich unserer Heimat einen grossen Dienst leistet, in dem sie das so rar gewordene Sohlleder sparen hilft." Arola Hauszeitung, no. 35, September 1943, p. 4.

11 "[...] eines ist sicher: die ganze Schweiz hat davon gesprochen und nicht zuletzt, dank verschiedener Angriffe gegen unseren 'Slogan.' Dass die ganze Sache allgemein schweizerisch bewertet wurde, beweisen die vielen humorvollen Beiträge im Nebelspalter, im Sie und Er und in verschiedenen anderen illustrierten Zeitungen, ganz abgesehen von vielen wertvollen Beiträgen aus der Feder von Journalisten und Modeschriftstellerinnen." Th.E. Kratzer in Arola Hauszeitung, no. 35, September 1943, p. 4.

12 Sudrow 2010, p. 319.

13 Arola Hauszeitung, no. 32, April 1942, p. 8.

14 Arola Hauszeitung, no. 41, December 1945, p. 60.

15 "Er eilt den Wandlungen der Zeit voraus und seine Kreationen erhalten dem Bally-Produkt das hohe Ansehen als internationaler Modeschuh", ibid., no. 38, January 1945, p. 5.

16 Federal Department of Economic Affairs (ed.) Der Schuhhandel in der Schweiz (Bern 1946) (publication of the Price Formation Commission of the Federal Department of Economic Affairs; 26), p. 31.

17 "Unsere überaus reiche Kollektion reizender, gesetzlich geschützter Bally-Kreationen ermöglichen Ihnen jede individuelle Wahl", advertisement for Bally Doelker, published April 3–5 April 1939 (Agor AG, dated checklists with advertisements for branches of Bally).

18 Agor AG, dated inspection sheets with advertisements for branches of Bally.

19 "[...] grosse, einflussreiche Tyrannin", Arola Hauszeitung, no. 32, April 1942, p. 6.

20 See Roman Wild's article in this volume, p. 21.

21 Arola Hauszeitung, no. 33, September/October 1942, p. 7.

22 "[...] unbescheidenen Ansprüche unserer Kunden", ibid., no. 32, April 1942, p. 6.

23 "Es ist unerlässlich, die Modebestrebungen mächtig zu unterstützen. Denn wenn z.B. in unseren Branchen jedes Geschäft nur einfache und einfachste Schuhe zeigen würde, würde ja bald die Frau weniger Paare kaufen. Die Mode will somit das Lustgefühl wecken, mehr zu kaufen", ibid., no. 34, March 1943, p. 24.

24 "Les effets de semelle plateforme et les talons lourds sont au goût du jour", ibid., no. 27, June 1940, p. 2.

25 There is no clear definition as to what constitutes a platform shoe. The Mode- und Kostümlexikon offers the following definition: "Shoes fitted with outer soles measuring several centimetres in height [...]" (Loschek 2011, p. 406).

26 Original quote in English. Semmelhack 2008, p. 42.

27 Chenoune 1995, p. 205.

28 "[...] mittels zusätzlicher alter Gummisohlen zum begehrten 'Doppelbock' [wurde]", Sultano 1995, p. 93.

29 McNeil/Riello 2006, pp. 94–115.

30 "Die moderne Frau trägt [...] den Glasabsatz mit eingebautem Goldfisch-Aquarium", Nebelspalter, no. 28, 9 July 1942, p. 7.

31 Sie und Er, no. 38, 1942, n.p. (summer fashion issue).

32 "Das blaue Band der Schweizer Qualität. Der Schuh aus Schönenwerd", Annabelle, no. 13, March 1939, p. 28.

33 Sie und Er, no. 17, 1942, p. 547.

34 "Worauf werden wir diesen Sommer gehen – auf Kork, Holz oder Stroh?" Sie und Er, no. 13, 1943, p. 418.

35 "Holz ist die grosse Mode", Sie und Er, no. 13, 1943, p. 31.

36 For more on the term and history, see Wolter 2003, pp. 18–38, particularly pp. 28–33.

37 https://de.wikipedia.org/wiki/Nebelspalter (accessed 29 February 2016).

38 "[...] jener Integrationsideologie, die Einheit von Volk und Staat propagierte und geprägt war durch eine intensive Selbstbesinnung auf das 'typisch Schweizerische' und die Abwehr des Fremden", Meier/Gysin 2003, p. 178.

39 "Mythologisierung der eigenen Vergangenheit", Ratschiller 2004, p. 87.

40 Gegen rote und braune Fäuste: 380 Zeichnungen, gesammelt aus den Nebelspalter-Jahrgängen 1932 bis 1948 (Rorschach 1949).

41 "[...] Hauptzweck besteht darin, witzig-unterhaltend zu sein", Wolter 2003, p. 38.

42 L'Illustré, no. 52, 28 December 1944, p. 16.

43 Wolter 2003, p. 30.

44 Martignette/Meisel 2002, p. 22.

45 Ibid., pp. 32–33.

46 Meier/Gysin 2003, p. 25.

47 Ibid., p. 214.

48 Ibid., p. 214.

49 "Die Frau weiss heute, dass sie damit rechnen muss, eventuell selbst militärisch herangezogen zu werden, dass sie aber gerade darum erst recht trachten muss, sich ihre Weiblichkeit und ihren Charme zu bewahren. Sie verzichtet auf unzeitgemäße Übertreibung betreffend Silhouette und Details und folgt bereitwillig einer Mode, die auf sympathische Weise in weicher weiblicher Linie eine unaufdringliche zukunftsgläubige Heiterkeit zum Ausdruck bringt", Arola Hauszeitung, no. 26, March 1940, p. 2.

50 Ineichen 2009, p. 31.

51 See, for example, the review of the guest performance by Jo Bouillon, described as a "specialist in swing and 'hot' swing", NZZ, 1 December 1941, p. 2.

52 "Ein Trost ist uns aber sicher: die Zeiten sind hart und die Swings können sich ihnen nicht entziehen. Eines Tages erhalten sie das Aufgebot zur Rekrutenschule, zum Luftschutz oder zur Landhilfe. Das Leben swingt dann mit ihnen in einer etwas rauheren, keineswegs missverständlichen Art. Aus diesem so ganz anders gearteten Swing gehen sie meistens mit klaren Augen und Beinen, die nicht mehr schlenkern, hervor," NZZ, 10 January 1943, p. 19.

53 Diner 2002, pp. 29–30.

54 Ibid., p. 30.

55 Bochsler 2015, p. 80.

56 Ibid., p. 86.

57 "[…] wobei das eigentlich beschämendste für unser Land [ist], dass hiebei die Schwarzen bei weitem bevorzugt [werden]", quoted in Bochsler 2006, p. 245.

58 http://www.hls-dhs-dss.ch/textes/d/D8704.php (accessed 1 March 2016).

59 Brändle 2013, pp. 177–178.

60 "Zum ersten Mal seit mehr als 100 Jahren kann man sich nicht mehr in Paris über die Mode informieren. […] Die Mode steht darob nicht still. Es gehen nur gewisse Verschiebungen vor sich, indem man sich 1. nach anderen Anregungsgelegenheiten umsieht, und indem 2. der Ausfall von Paris unversehens zum Ansporn wird, mehr selbständiges eigenes Können zu

entfalten. Bezeichnenderweise wird dabei in keinem Land an eine eigenbrödlerische, national gefärbte Mode gedacht. Im Gegenteil. [...] Der Gedanke etwa an eine 'schweizerische Mode' wird auch bei uns grundsätzlich gar nicht diskutiert", Arola Hauszeitung, no. 28, September 1940, p. 1.

61 For example, see Junker, Almut. Frankfurt Macht Mode 1933–1945 (Marburg 1999); Guenther, Irene. Nazi Chic? Fashioning Women in the Third Reich (Oxford 2004).

62 For example, see Veillon, Dominique. La mode sous l'occupation (Paris, 1990).

63 For example, see Griffith, Suzanne. Stitching for Victory (Stroud 2009); Sultano, Gloria. Wie geistiges Kokain. Mode unterm Hakenkreuz (Vienna 1995); Summers, Julie. Fashion on the Ration: Style in the Second World War (London 2015).

Schönenwerd—New York
Bally Evening Shoes

Katharina Tietze

It is remarkable how many extravagant evening shoes dating from the 1930s are to be found in the company archives of the Swiss shoe firm *Bally:* shoes with elegant heels, in gold or silver leather with pale blue grosgrain fabric or red satin, decorated with delicate stitching or rhinestone buckles. Most of the shoes, especially from the first half of the century, are similar in form [FIG. 1].

The heels are moderately high, and the toes rounded: heels and toes tend to be enclosed, and narrow straps support the foot. Later on, towards the end of the decade, one or two sandals appear which leave the foot more exposed, together with the occasional platform shoe. What is remarkable about the shoes, and typical of *Bally,* is the high quality of the workmanship and the artistry of the detailing and the decorative elements. Of the approximately 600 ladies' shoes in the shoe archive dating from the 1930s, 241 can be categorized as evening shoes—more than one third. Even a very elegant lady

[1] Evening shoes by Bally, 1930s
(Historical Archives of Bally Schuhfabriken AG; photo: Manuel Fabritz, © Bally)

would not have had such a high proportion of evening shoes in her wardrobe. Why are there so many luxurious shoes in a period which falls between the start of the Great Depression in 1929 and the outbreak of the Second World War in 1939? How can this collection of costly objects be analyzed and categorized? For whom were the elegant shoes intended?

As the price lists for shoes produced for Switzerland show,[1] these styles were not made for home consumption. In most of the lists, evening shoes are shown in a category of their own, but they are very much simpler in design and made of less expensive materials. The styles are more enclosed; in fact, most of the shoes are pumps. There is also a complete absence of coloured fabric and much less decoration. The shoes are mainly black, sometimes trimmed with gold or silver leather.

The elegant evening shoes, then, were intended for export. Ever since its foundation in 1851, *Bally* had been geared towards international sales; the Swiss market was too small for sustained commercial success. In the 1920s and 1930s, once the company had become well established in the German, French, and British markets,[2] capturing the US market became an important objective. Though promisingly large, however, this was a market with exacting quality standards, America being the world leader in shoe production.

It is my contention that *Bally* captured the US market with high-fashion shoes, of which the luxurious ladies' shoes in the company archives are examples. Did these shoes, then, match up to elegant New York society's standards of high fashion? Is there any evidence of *Bally* shoes in the USA? And what proof is there of commercial ties? These are the questions I shall be investigating in this chapter.

"21 Pairs of Shoes"

By the 1930s, shoes were already receiving a lot of attention in the American edition of *Vogue,* in both editorials and advertisements. European fashion periodicals, on the other hand, still hardly ever mentioned shoes. There were practically no articles about them in *die neue linie,* an avant-garde magazine with artwork by famous Bauhaus designers such as László Moholy-Nagy and Herbert Bayer. The same is true of *Elegante Welt,* a conservative German publication of the same period. Even in the Swiss *Annabelle,* which first appeared in 1938, there was only the occasional mention of footwear.

A good example of how important a topic shoes were for American *Vogue* is an article published in April 1930. Entitled "21 Pairs of Shoes", it declared that all of the following 21 pairs of shoes were to be found in the well-dressed woman's wardrobe: "Eight are for general daytime wear, morning and afternoon. Seven are for sportswear, both active and spectator variety. The evening group includes four, the boudoir group two."[3] The article takes up seven pages. On the first, the shoes are pictured in a wardrobe; then each one is illustrated again individually. Likewise, the shoes are described in detail, both in the text and in the picture captions. Comparing the evening shoes illustrated here with those from the *Bally* company archives, one finds almost identical styles [FIGS. IIA, IIB]. The evening-shoe group includes two pairs of sandals with ankle straps and enclosed toes, one, from Delman,[4] in silk with a narrow gold-leather strap, the other in silver brocade with a blue sheen and silver leather trim, from Altman. Also recommended are two pairs of evening pumps, one shoe described as a "classic opera pump"[5] in black

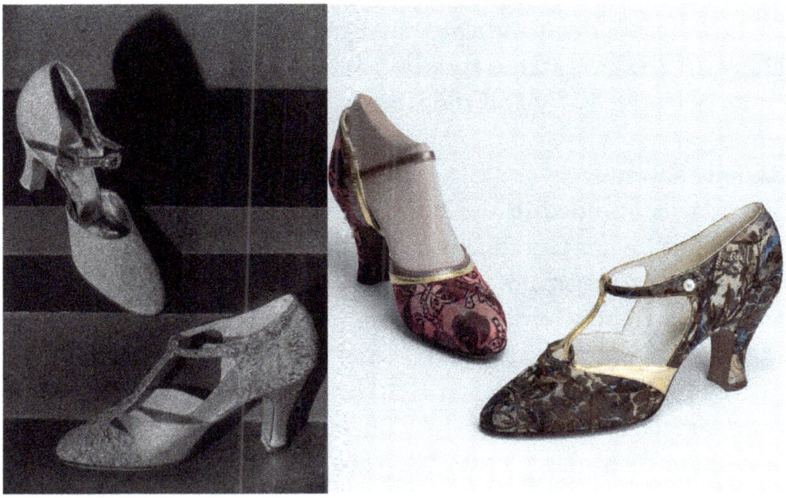

[IIA, IIB] Evening sandals, 1930
(American Vogue, 12 April 1930, p. 104, © Condé Nast / Historical Archives of Bally Schuhfabriken AG; photo: Manuel Fabritz, © Bally)

satin with a buckle and the other in white crêpe de Chine trimmed with gold and silver leather. The "boudoir" group comprises a peach-coloured satin slipper with an embroidered name and a pair of "Greek" evening sandals with gold straps, which give the foot the appearance of being almost bare. Only for these more frivolous boudoir styles is it harder to find *Bally* equivalents; for example, it was not until much later, in 1947, that the company produced a similar satin slipper.

It is clear that the *Bally* shoes are perfectly comparable with those illustrated in the *Vogue* article. What's more, the comparison highlights the potential of the *Bally* collection: shoes of which only poor-quality black-and-white images now remain can be compared with real objects. Moreover, the article puts the evening shoe in the context of the many different styles of ladies' shoe available at the time and the appropriate occasions for wearing them.

American *Vogue* is a rich source for analyzing shoe fashions. My research into the history of shoes involves examining barely discernible details in printed black-and-white photos from the 1930s. Fortunately, every edition of *Vogue* is available online with a picture quality as good as that of the printed versions.

I will first give an idea of how evening shoes are presented in American *Vogue* and then analyze the appearances of *Bally* shoes in the magazine; finally, I will look at the commercial links between *Bally* and the American market.

Shoe Fashion

Vogue was founded in 1892 in the USA. In 1907, it was bought by the publisher Condé Nast, which turned it into the first modern women's magazine. Condé Nast increased the circulation tenfold, attracted more advertising, and succeeded in making the magazine a financial success. The first British edition appeared in 1916, followed in 1920 by the French edition. Today there are 21 different editions. The editor-in-chief in the 1930s was Edna Woolman Chase. She was in charge of the magazine for 37 years, from 1914 to 1951.

In the 1930s, *Vogue* appeared every two weeks, with over 100 pages in each edition. Even in those days, a large proportion of the pages were advertisements, and alongside cars and cosmetics these also included adverts for shoes.

One edition in 1930, for example, contained ten full-page shoe adverts, mostly placed by shoe shops and large department stores. In approximately every third magazine there were editorials with shoes as their subject.

Looking through the magazines from the 1930s is like time travel; a whole world opens up. First-rate creative minds worked for *Vogue:* Cecil Beaton wrote, drew, and photographed; there are short stories by Dorothy Parker, and photographs by Man Ray and Horst P. Horst. The product is extraordinarily creative and diverse; in its mixture of illustrations and photographs, its detailed texts, its layout, every opportunity for innovative fashion reporting is exploited. Each cover, for example, integrates the *Vogue* logo into the title picture in a different way. At the same time, the magazine gives the reader a valuable insight into the style-conscious urban upper class of America of the 1930s.

For illustrating how shoe fashion was presented in the magazine, the pictures of one of the magazine's contributors, the renowned and multi-talented photographer, Edward Steichen, are particularly revealing. Born in 1879 and raised in Milwaukee, Steichen began to work for *Vogue* in 1923 and left the magazine in 1937. The first-ever use of colour photography on the front cover of *Vogue* in 1932 was of his work. His photographs of shoes not only convey an impression of shoe fashion of the 1930s, they show his mastery of innovative staging. They clearly demonstrate that the way in which fashion is illustrated in magazines is itself part of fashion. The poet Carl Sandburg, Steichen's brother-in-law, said that, for him, "many of the photographs of shoes he took for *Vogue* have just as great an aesthetic value as the photographs of roses or foxgloves on which he lavished all his skill and creativity".[6] Every photograph by Steichen appears with his name, showing just how seriously he took his work on social and fashion photography.

A one-page article devoted exclusively to evening shoes appeared in January 1930 [FIG. III]. Steichen approached the shoes like precious objects, so that the shots were not cluttered, with the shoes commanding the space around them. The most striking aspect of his photograph is the exaggerated interplay of light and shadow, making the shoes appear like objects projected by the light and producing a variety of reflections from their different materials in the photographic print.

A detailed eight-page article discusses beauty treatment for various parts of the body; the tips for face, hands, and feet are illustrated with full-page photos by Steichen and small drawings [FIG. IV]. The photo for the feet is astonishing for its feeling of timeless modernity; like other photos in the series, it has a captivating sculptural simplicity: naked legs stretch upwards, clothed only in a pair of flat Roman sandals. No other items of clothing appear in any of this series of photos; it is only the feet which are not left bare.

The advice given by the article consists of tips for keeping one's body conditioned through sport and maintaining a smooth complexion—the sort of advice still typical today. The last section ("Make them up") begins: "The more feet and legs show, the more beautiful they must be made." There

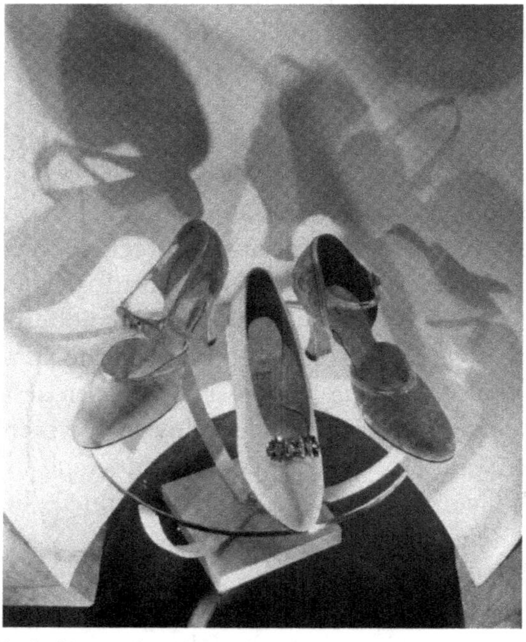

[III] Photo: Edward Steichen
(American Vogue, 30 January 1930, p. 58, © Condé Nast)

follows a detailed explanation of what a pedicure is and why it flatters the feet. The article is evidence of the fact that sandals were becoming more and more fashionable, both for the beach and for evening wear, with bare legs, manicured feet and varnished toenails becoming correspondingly more topical. Nevertheless, the occasions on which women might show their toes were still strictly regulated. In 1939 an article appeared under the defiant title, "Vogue Protests! Open Toes and Open Heels Are Not for City Streets."[7]

In another article with photos by Steichen, the shoes are worn by models. In all the pictures, hands and feet appear in elegant pictorial compositions. The different textures of clothes, furniture, carpet fabrics, jewellery, and even a dog's fur contrast with and contextualize the shoes. The article, "Fashionable Extremities of Ten Smart Women", goes so far as to name the women who have chosen and are wearing the shoes. "Each photograph is [...] the individual 'shoe-cast' of a fashionable woman who knows what she likes and likes what is smart [...]."[8] The photo shows the feet of Princess Paley.

[IV] Photo: Edward Steichen
(American Vogue, 1 June 1934, p. 46, © Condé Nast)

Edward Steichen's photographs demonstrate the change in the way fashion trends were transmitted. He experimented with light, cropped images, models, and new technologies. The sophistication of his black-and-white photography fills even a modern viewer with admiration.

In the first half of the 1930s, sandals were fashionable both for the beach and for evening wear, but in the second half of the decade, platform soles and wedge heels completely altered shoe styles. This had an interesting, diversifying effect on evening-shoe styles as well; new heel shapes were introduced, and the foot became increasingly exposed.

Bally* in *Vogue

In 1929, before the first appearance of *Bally* shoes in *Vogue* magazine, the new *Bally* shoe shop in Paris was featured; an illustration shows the elegant Art Deco façade, designed by Robert Mallet-Stevens.[9]

Between 1936 and 1941, there are altogether eleven illustrations of *Bally* shoes, mostly drawings in editorial articles on shoe fashion. After this, no *Bally* shoes are mentioned until 1947, when they appear again in the context of ski shoes, in anticipation of the Winter Olympics to be held that year in St. Moritz. Then there is another gap, until the firm itself placed advertisements in *Vogue* for the first time in the 1950s. Of course, *Bally* shoes can only be identified in the magazines of the 1930s if they are named as such in the picture captions. In an exhibition on Horst P. Horst at the Victoria & Albert Museum, I found evidence that other *Bally* shoes were also illustrated. According to the exhibition cat-

[VA, VB] Ladies' shoes by Bally, 1940
(American Vogue, 1 January 1940, p. 80, © Condé Nast/Historical Archives of Bally Schuhfabriken AG; photo: Manuel Fabritz, © Bally)

alogue, a mannequin modelling a tunic by Alix was wearing shoes by *Bally,* although this is not mentioned in the magazine.[10] We can assume, therefore, that shoes were matched with clothes as suitable accessories without being named in the picture captions. In terms of style, material, and function, *Vogue* presented many different types of shoe in its articles; in the case of *Bally* shoes, these included not just evening shoes, but also sandals. In July 1936, summer fashions are presented under the heading "Midsummer"; a double spread shows a bird's eye view of models reclining in a meadow.[11] Two of them are wearing identical linen sandals by *Bally,* simple summer shoes made of a light-coloured material with a low heel. These are possibly the *Hospodarsky* sandals, named after their inventor, *Bally's* chief designer. A quarter of a million of this style were sold to North America between 1923 and 1941.[12] In 1940, we find sandals again, this time in white material trimmed with blue leather.

Bally shoes with modest heels are also illustrated for daywear, many of them featuring unusual details or materials. "Shoemaking is a plastic art", declares an article in the August 1938 edition.[13] The flexibility and sculptural qualities of the new shoes are the main focus of the discussion. Amongst the

VOGUE
SEEN IN SAINT MORITZ
After skiing, Mademoiselle Chanel puts on these Bally boots, which she bought in Saint Moritz. A white leather pair with a blue knitted cuff and red laces. A black calf pair, white-laced

[VI] "Seen in Saint Moritz"
(American Vogue, 15 January 1939, p. 94, © Condé Nast)

illustrations are two styles by *Bally:* a buckle shoe, "soft as a slipper", made of blue suede, and an opera pump in wine-red suede with ruched detailing. In January 1940, shoes in red and white are featured [FIGS. VA, VB]. The white lace-up shoe from *Bally* has a so-called "tractor" heel covered in red shagreen. In the *Bally* archives there is a very similar shoe, albeit in brown and without the laces. Shagreen was experimented with in Europe when cow and calf-leather were in short supply as a result of the Second World War. A by-product of the food industry, it was used as a substitute for reptile leather.[14] A buckle shoe from *Bally* "for every day and all day long" is featured in 1940.

And in autumn 1941, in an article on black shoes, a *Bally* lacing shoe made of fur and suede is illustrated.[15] Here, too, there is a very similar shoe, in the same combination of materials, in the *Bally* archives. Naturally, there could not fail to be a mention of ski boots: a small article in the winter of 1939 recommends Switzerland as an exclusive country in which to holiday [FIG. VI]. When Coco Chanel wears *Bally* on a skiing holiday, even functional shoes look glamorous.

Last but not least, *Bally* evening shoes were also featured in *Vogue;* for instance, the above-mentioned evening pumps. In 1940, *Vogue* featured an illustration of a linen evening shoe of unusual design; it envelops the ankle and is almost a hybrid of a summer sandal and an evening shoe.[16] The 1939 article entitled "American Mania" features an evening sandal [FIGS. VIIA, VIIB]. The material is described as "black 'cellophane' cloth fired with gold kid". In the *Bally* archives there

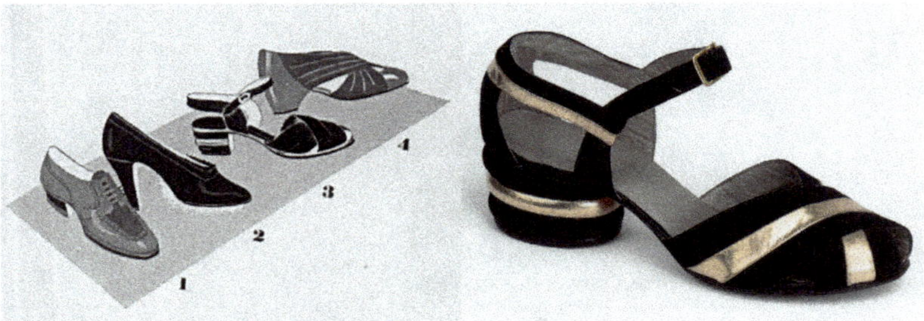

[VIIA, VIIB] Sandals by Bally, 1939
(American Vogue, 1 February 1939, p. 111, © Condé Nast/Historical Archives of Bally Schuhfabriken AG; photo: Manuel Fabritz, © Bally)

is a very similar shoe; in this case, however, black suede is used. The shape of the heel is interesting, being reminiscent of a famous shoe designed for Judy Garland for a stage and film production in 1938, allegedly as a one-off: for the platform heels, Salvatore Ferragamo had covered individual cork layers with suede of different colours; the *Bally* shoe quotes this ridged-layer effect. This clearly shows how closely *Bally* followed international shoe fashion and imitated its trends, even if the new styles were reproduced in a very much more restrained form.

In the *Bally* archives there are three other models with similar heels, and in the Costume Institute of the Metropolitan Museum in New York there is a shoe which is identical to one of them, apart from being a different colour—a dark rose [FIG. VIII]. *Bally* shoes were thus not only endorsed in the USA, but also worn, treasured, and preserved.

Commercial Relations

"In terms of numbers, the USA was at the peak of its shoe production and consumption at the start of the 1930s",[17] writes

[VIII] Evening sandal by Bally, 1939
(Historical Archives of Bally Schuhfabriken AG; photo: Manuel Fabritz, © Bally)

Anne Sudrow in her impressive study on the shoe under National Socialism. *Bally* was one of those companies which, early on, took inspiration from the American industrialization of shoe production. In 1876, Eduard Bally, the son of the firm's founder, travelled to the first American international exhibition in Philadelphia and brought new machines back with him. The mechanization of shoe production in the USA was a reaction to the demand of a rapidly growing population. Other reasons for the USA's pioneering role in the industry were that shoe sizes were standardized there as early as 1886, and the country was rich in raw materials.

Bally had a sales agency in New York from 1923, and in 1930 it took over a children's shoe factory in Philadelphia. From 1919 to 1929, sales of *Bally* shoes in the USA rose from zero to 295,144 pairs.[18] Trade relations then fell victim to the effects of the Great Depression, in the wake of which protective tariffs, including tariffs on shoes, were introduced in 1930. From 1935 onwards, sales began to increase slightly again, until the outbreak of the Second World War once more made conditions difficult.[19] Nevertheless, 54,482 pairs were exported to the USA in 1940/41.[20] At this point, the USA was *Bally's* third largest market, after Germany and France.

Switzerland, conversely, was also respected by the USA, both as a competitor and as a market. In 1926, a report by the US Department of Commerce, entitled "Switzerland: Resources, Industries, and Trade", concluded that Switzerland deserved a great deal more attention than might be supposed from its size and population.[21]

In 1942, *Bally's* house journal, *Bally Mitteilungen,* explained to employees in Switzerland the company's success in the USA:

> With all due respect to the US shoe industry, it may be said that our products still lead the way with respect to detail. From a purely technical point of view, marvelous things are being achieved over there, but the meticulous care we take with uppers, seaming, silks, leather piping, and ornamentation, as beautifully finished as haute couture products, is not something one encounters in American shoe ranges.[22]

And in 1944, the quality of the workmanship was emphasized again: "What we have been manufacturing up to now for the USA have been very expensive ladies' shoes, characterized by tasteful styles, exquisite raw materials and the superior workmanship of their soles and uppers."[23]

Surprisingly, people on the American side came to much the same conclusion, a fact that also speaks for the quality of the *Bally* house magazine. In 1932, a report by the United States Tariff Commission, entitled "Boots and Shoes", compared US products with imports. The shoes were categorized according to manufacturing technique, and the report recognized Swiss shoes as representing competition for American products in the "turned"[24] category for light women's shoes and children's shoes. The report notes: "Some of the imported shoes may have more fancy stitching and appliqué, foxing or inserts, than the ordinary domestic article, but the two are unquestionably competitive."[25] *Bally* is reckoned by the report to be by far the largest shoe producer in Switzerland, manufacturing practically all the shoes which were exported to the USA, and around 80 percent of shoe exports from Switzerland overall. Here is confirmation that it was the cutting-edge ladies' shoe which would capture the American market. There would be many difficulties to overcome along the way, however. Also in *Bally Mitteilungen,* we find an article by a certain P. Hünerwadel, reporting on his first journey through the USA as a company rep in 1922.[26] He travelled with a collection of 200 shoes, which had to be unpacked and packed up again twenty times in order to find takers for them among the leading department stores and businesses. It was not only difficult to find sales outlets; the sizing had to meet American expectations, and, above all, deliveries had to be prompt. American buyers were used to reordering successful styles four weeks after the start of the season, but it took time for these to reach New York by steamship. Nevertheless, it was important to capture this market. Ivan Bally, a grandson of the company's founder, stressed as early as 1932: "For Switzerland there always has been, and there continues to be, an absolute necessity to export."[27] This requirement became even more pressing during the Second World War; as circumstances became increasingly difficult in Europe, the USA was seen as being the market of the future. It was a challenge the *Bally* company set out to meet.

The *Bally* evening shoes which were sold in the 1930s in the USA not only met North-American commercial standards but also the standards of fashion. The sources in the company archives and the articles in *Vogue* complement one another as proof of this: The shoes in the archive provide abundant concrete examples, while the editorial articles contextualize them in word and picture, and, again and again, precise correspondences between them can be found. *Bally* shoes shone, quite literally, by virtue of their exquisite detailing and high standard of workmanship. Documents from the archives, moreover, give an idea of how *Bally* went about capturing the American market and the difficulties it encountered in doing so. Clearly, great importance was attached to high-fashion evening shoes as products for sale to America. By following the journey of a brilliant Swiss product across the Atlantic to New York, we can thus trace an important stage in the development of the 20th century fashion shoe.

1 The catalogues appeared half-yearly; all of them are present in the archives, except for the summer catalogue for 1933. In all the catalogues, apart from those for 1932, 1932/33, and 1943, evening shoes are listed separately. From 1942 until the end of the war, there were only two styles; previously there had been around ten, and in 1937/38 there were as many as 19 different styles.

2 [Author unknown] 1951. Retail companies belonging to the Bally holding company were founded in 1906 in Berlin, 1908 in London, 1917 in Paris, 1921 in Brussels, and 1923 in New York.

3 American Vogue, 12 April 1930, p. 103.

4 One of the oldest US shoe brands still in existence today, founded in 1919 by Herman Delman.

5 American Vogue, 12 April 1930, p. 122.

6 Niven 1997, p. 536.

7 American Vogue, 1 July 1939, pp. 58f.

8 Ibid., 1 March 1935, p. 73.

9 Ibid., 22 June 1929, p. 53.

10 Brown 2014, p. 84.

11 American Vogue, 15 July 1936, pp. 28f.

12 [Author unknown] 1941, p. 8.

13 American Vogue, 1 August 1938, pp. 86f. For both shoes, Lawrence Parker is named as the importer.

14 Sudrow 2010, p. 270.

15 American Vogue, 1 September 1940, p. 118.

16 Ibid., "New Camel Colors", February 15, 1940, pp. 87f.

17 Sudrow 2010, p. 31.

18 Straub 1942, p. II.

19 Ibid., p. III.

20 [Author unknown] 1942.

21 Tanner 2015, p. 177.

22 Straub 1942, p. III.

23 Kamber 1944, p. VII.

24 Sole and upper are sewn with right sides together and then turned, so that the seams are on the inside of the shoe.

25 United States Tariff Commission 1932, p. 15.

26 Hünerwadel 1944, p. II.

27 Bally 1932, no page no.

Functional Shoes

The Development of Utility Shoes,[1] Their Differentiation and Interfaces with Fashion

Daniel Späti

Two developments in the late 19th and early 20th century appear to have provided an important basis for subsequent designs. In the 19th century, a movement initiated by anatomists resulted in the launch of the *shoe reform*,[2] which aimed to apply ergonomic and orthopedic knowledge to footwear design. This put shoe manufacturing for the first time on an entirely scientific footing. The military made a significant contribution to the practical implementation and international spread of the shoe reform, since good footwear played a critical role in an army's readiness for war. The Swiss army's *Model 1892* was constructed in accordance with the guiding principles of "rational shoe design".

The second crucial development was the *change in shoe usage*. At the beginning of the 20th century, the average inhabitant of the German-speaking world typically owned just one pair of shoes, sometimes with a second for Sunday best.[3] In general, a high premium was placed on the sturdiness of footwear, which wearers expected to be durable and readily reparable. This often meant a mid-calf lace-up boot, worn essentially as all-round or multifunctional footwear. For men, the choice of footwear was likely limited to black lace-up boots [FIG. 1].

During the 1920s, the German-speaking world underwent a massive shift in the most commonly worn type of footwear, with shoes replacing lace-up boots.[4] People increasingly lived in cities where streets were better developed, making it possible to opt for lighter footwear. Whereas there was minimal variation in the choice of lace-up boots (at least in terms of appearance), shoes—particularly for women—quickly evolved into a diverse range of fashionable varieties. However, the fast pace of fashion meant that such shoes were often made to a poorer quality and were also less easy to repair.[5] In general terms, it is possible to observe the shoe's value in use losing significance in favour of its qualities as a fashion item, while increasing industrialization lowered production costs and allowed rates of shoe consumption to increase many times over.[6]

These near-identical posters, albeit separated by four intervening years, show the transformation of uniform mountain-hiking footwear to a casual shoe that women could pair with increasingly fashionable clothing [FIGS. II, III].

Development and Differentiation of the Practical Utility Shoe

Technological development and new opportunities for leisure activities led to the increasing differentiation of utility footwear, particularly in the realm of sport. This was the period that saw the establishment of sports footwear companies such as Adidas (1924) and Puma (1948); skiing and Alpine tourism became more and more accessible to the mass market,[7] while rubber soles began their onward march to dominance. However, footwear designed for functional purposes remained "for the time being largely unaffected by the trends of fashion".[8]

The *lace-up boot* continued to be the basic design for many types of practical utility footwear [FIG. IV]. It remained the most

[I] Bally poster 1927; Hugo Laubi
(Historical Archives of Bally Schuhfabriken AG)

common variety of everyday footwear until 1920—typically available in brown or black, and boasting a solid and readily repairable construction. Variations existed primarily in the choice of material and type of construction (usually the "Derby" construction,[9] ideally double-stitched).[10] Footwear of this kind was only lightly studded (if at all), and featured at most discreet decorative seams or other forms of subtle ornamentation.

For *work shoes*, there were one or two differentiations in design depending on the practical use they served; generally, however, they were lace-up boots, with shafts that came slightly above ankle-height. The boots were available in black and made using extremely robust material, with construction geared entirely to maximizing longevity. Owners would probably have had to wear in the boot for quite some time until it fitted the foot properly and felt more comfortable. The majority of work boots, depending on their function, would have been studded with a greater or lesser degree of intricacy.

The Swiss army's mid-length lace-up *marching boot*[11] underwent a series of incremental developments of varying scale between 1930 and 1960. One noteworthy example was the introduction of the rubber sole in around 1954.[12] At the same

[II] Bally poster, 1924;
Emil Cardinaux (Historical Archives of Bally Schuhfabriken AG)

[III] Bally poster, 1928;
Emil Cardinaux (Historical Archives of Bally Schuhfabriken AG)

time, shoes with studded leather soles continued to be both produced and worn. This was in part a consequence of the large quantity of stocks still available, although it also provided a way of supporting the shoemaking trade, which was not equipped to manufacture rubber soles and had become increasingly focused on producing boots for officers, who paid out of their own pocket. Difficulties in procuring materials during wartime scarcity meant that the shaft height of the 1941 model was reduced by 1.5 cm.[13] Thanks to its high quality and the policy of providing all soldiers with a free pair, the military boot often made its way into civilian life as work footwear. In contrast to the men's boot, the model worn by the Swiss Women's Auxiliary Service in this period already had a subtly fashionable touch: produced in brown with a red seam, the boot even featured some light padding.

Walking and *climbing boots* are related both in their construction and design to work and marching footwear: lace-up boots with a relatively low shaft, boasting leather lining and felt cloth to prevent the leather from cutting into the foot. Furthermore, they all boast a high-drawn lined tongue, sturdy soles, and resilient material. The more stress the boots were made to withstand, the stronger they became. At *Bally*, "climbing boots had to represent the best in comfort, water resistance, and fit".[14] The most obvious differentiating feature of these various boots was usually their soles or the formation of their studs. The latter lent the sole both grip and longevity, since it protected the sole leather from wear and, when necessary, could also be replaced.

[IV] Bally lace-up boots between 1920 and 1930 (Historical Archives of Bally Schuhfabriken AG; photo: Manuel Fabritz, © Bally)

Available in a number of shapes and sizes, they varied from the lighter outsoles used for everyday footwear, to the sturdier varieties typical of work shoes, and the heavy outsoles fitted onto mountain boots [FIG. V].

Alpine expeditions require boot soles to have excellent traction in order to give wearers enhanced protection from slipping. To achieve this, studdings such as the *Grenacher* and *Bernina,*[15] then subsequently the *Tricouni,* were developed.[16] The latter was created in around 1912 by a Geneva jeweller and passionate mountain climber, and is still produced today in Bulle, Switzerland. The studding gave wearers excellent footing, although the metal plates at the heel in particular acted as cold conductors. For this reason, *Bally* experimented with vulcanized *Sparta* rubber soles for its Alpine climbing boots. These responded exceptionally well to the challenges they were put through, including the need to remain reliably waterproof. However, the greatest advantage was that the same boot was suited to both the approaches and ascents that characterize mountaineering climbs.[17] *Bally* provided the equipment for a number of expeditions to the Himalayas, most famously for the first ascent of Mount Everest in 1953, for which Tenzing Norgay was supplied with *Bally* reindeer-lined boots (a fact the company continues to publicize to this day). The 1940s and 1950s witnessed the creation of a large number of modifications that anticipated future

[V] Bally climbing boots (Grenacher and Tricouni outsoles on left and right respectively) 1930–40 (Historical Archives of Bally Schuhfabriken AG; photo: Manuel Fabritz, © Bally)

developments, such as better padded climbing boots, lighter-weight hiking boots, and their more distant relatives, après-ski boots.

Climbing and hiking boots also fall into the category of *sports footwear,* a sector that grew with particular dynamism during these decades. An article published in 1928 in *Das Werk* magazine vaunted this development:

> Sports footwear is probably the branch of the large Swiss maker of quality products, the Bally shoe manufacturers, that represents a quintessentially modern creation. Shoes for street and evening wear are developments of pre-existing types of footwear. Sports footwear, by contrast, embodies an avowedly modern concept both in terms of function and design.[18]

Existing footwear was increasingly differentiated while new types were created, including designs for tennis, track and field, ice-skating, ice hockey, soccer—as well as hunting and fishing.

Shoes and Functionality

The concept of the "functionality" of products and their design is subject to constant debate. The term is modified and expanded, then matched to the developments and requirements that emerge out of technological and social change. An understanding of a product's function is today given a fundamentally broad footing and understood as a complex network. It is possible to glean a good insight into changing design criteria over the course of the 20th century by reference to the utility shoe's differentiation and evolution through fashion.

Only limited literature is available on the theme of "functionality and shoes". As Anne Sudrow has written, shoes generally fulfill the following basic requirements:

1. Protection of foot from injury, dirt and cold, heat, and other atmospheric conditions;
2. Providing cover from the "indiscreet gaze"; clothing that functions as a second skin, delineating the body from surrounding space;
3. Decoration and accentuation of body (which is equally fundamental).[19]

As design functions diversified, protection of the foot came increasingly under the aegis of practical considerations. Meanwhile, cover from the "indiscreet gaze", as well as features for decorating and accentuating the foot, became categorized as more emotional functions. Christoph Ebert designates and outlines the factors for assessing sports footwear's functionality by reference to three levels:

1. Basic factors: These encompass functions that result in dissatisfaction when they do not meet the sportsperson's corresponding expectations. If the sportsperson has a positive awareness of them, this still does not lead to satisfaction, but rather to mere "non-dissatisfaction". These minimal requirements thus relate to the sports product's core performances.
2. Performance factors: These relate to functions that can lead both to satisfaction when the customer's expectations are exceeded, and to dissatisfaction when the sportsperson's expectations are not met.
3. Inspirational factors: These relate to functions that result in satisfaction when they are available to the sportsperson, but not necessarily to dissatisfaction when not. Inspirational features are not expected by the sportsperson and therefore serve to heighten the experience of a core performance.[20]

Functionality Using the Example of the Ski Boot

In the following section, I will use the example of the ski boot to undertake a somewhat closer examination of the practical and technical functionality of a type of utility footwear. A brief survey of the history of the ski boot's development shows that skis were not originally viewed as sports equipment, but were instead used for mobility in regions prone to heavy snowfall. It was Alpine ski pioneers who first designed equipment for the rigors of downhill skiing. As a result of the development of *Lilienfeld ski binding*,[21] the ski boot had to be made significantly more rigid in order to benefit from the improved lateral support this innovation provided. Since there were no ski lifts at the turn of the 20th century, the ski boot also had to be suitable for climbing.[22] The climbing boot initially served as the basis for the design, adapted through a variety of reinforcements and technical refinements: A heightened shaft, an inner shoe, and leather straps improved the boot's support, while special flat rubber soles enhanced its hold on the ski. Padding or inner leather soles measuring up to 2 cm in thickness offered improved comfort and helped protect the wearer from cold; overlapping tongue flaps and the use of treated materials made the boot waterproof. In the early 20th century, however, improvised adjustments continued to be the norm—wearers would strike nails into their mountain and walking boots, for example, as a way of preventing the binding straps from slipping over the heel.[23]

The footwear's development into a genuine ski boot took a while, although the expanding sportswear industry was constantly developing new, technically refined models at a tremendous rate. There soon emerged further differentiations of ski boots, as special models were created specifically for touring, piste, slalom, cross country, and downhill skiing.[24] The growing influence of "taste, fashion, and purchasing power"[25] was an additional driving force behind the increasing range of products.

An item of sports footwear should be constructed in a way that ensures it is equal to the particular demands of the sport, and equipped to deal with whatever "walking, running, stretching, jumping, and sliding movements"[26] the activity entails. For ski boots, the aim is to achieve a unity of foot, boot, and ski; to achieve this, every element must be optimally tailored. The upper leather should be "soft, supple, and waterproof, although at the same time it should also be able to dry as quickly as possible and allow the foot to perspire naturally as it is put through its paces".[27] Calf leather, a rather warm and hardy material, was the preferred choice for the leather lining. The alternative was (cheaper, thinner) goat leather—a less durable material, which heavy perspiration can cause to perish rapidly. During the 1940s, opinions were divided as to whether ski boots should have leather or rubber soles. There were two main types of construction: "screwed and duplicated"[28] by machine, or "double stitched" by craftsmen with some mechanical assistance.[29] The increasing scarcity of leather during the Second World War also influenced the manner in which ski boots were constructed; the shortage led to a ban on "seamless ski boots, straps for the instep and ankle, and strips of tire material around the top of the boot shaft", with only "material-saving shaft designs" permitted.[30] Nevertheless, Switzerland stood in marked contrast to neighbouring countries for it was at least still able to afford producing ski boots during these years.

Christoph Ebert cites in his study the essential requirements for ensuring the ski boot's practical and technical functionality. These stipulate (among other criteria) that the boot should:

- Facilitate walking
- Provide stability
- Transfer power
- Store warmth
- Repel water
- Enable movement[31]

In principle, many of these requirements also applied to the ski boots from the years around 1930, although they are measured differently today, and manufacturers have new technologies at their disposal. Over the years the ski boot has also become laden with elements designed to appeal to fashion tastes and to hold emotional, aesthetic, and symbolic values.

Fashionable Ski Boots

Although fashion still only wielded minimal influence over utility and sports footwear in the early 20th century, its influence increased considerably over the course of the 1930s and 1940s, and resulted in further differentiation.

In skiing, the rise of fashion trends was played out between "the respective poles of material expediency and social communication".[32] The (earlier) development of everyday footwear from boot to fashionable shoe inevitably spilled over and affected other types of shoe as well. Thanks to the significant growth in tourism (attracting large numbers of visitors from throughout the world), increasing amounts of leisure time, and rising prosperity, skiing developed from a pursuit practiced by men and women in small rural communities to a "lifestyle sport" undertaken as a social experience, for which outward appearances played a more significant role. A press release for the 1935 *Bally Sports Shoe Exhibition* in Zürich recounts this shift:

> The first of the larger sports footwear exhibitions took place in 1919, garnering highly favourable reports in the contemporary press. In the 16 years that have followed, tremendous progress has been made in the production of sports footwear. Since then, sport has conquered significant swathes of everyday life, taking on gigantic proportions in the process. One needs only look to skiing to see this […]. The factory houses a section devoted to […] its sports footwear collection that incorporates not only the latest technical innovations, but also the fashion trends that accompany them to an unprecedented extent. After all, sport nowadays does not just equate to "serious" sporting pursuits in which participants aim to score points, but can also refer to what is known as "fashionable sport". People take up a sport for the simple reason that it is in fashion. While […] for serious sports it is vital to ensure […] a level of quality that is up to the demands […] made by the sport in all circumstances, and to equip the wearer for all technical and weather-related conditions, for people concerned about the more fashion-related elements of the ensemble, it is imperative for the boot to coordinate with the overall outfit.[33]

[VI] Ski shoes, 1930–1950
(Historical Archives of Bally Schuhfabriken AG; photo: Manuel Fabritz, © Bally)

In the article, Hengartner also stresses how female customers in particular created "significant demand for imaginative tailoring and colourful ski boots". As he goes on to explain, "the beauty and elegance of this ski boot model later gave the impetus for the design and development of the après-ski model, which as we know can be seen being worn not only in winter sports resorts, but in our cities as well".[34] The foreground of a contemporary poster features the brown ski boot model for men, with one black and one multicoloured model for women shown in the background.

There emerged a distinction in ski boots between strictly functional models designed specifically for sport and a more fashionable line. *Bally* released models "both for the lone skier who ventures over canyons, glaciers, and virgin snow at an altitude of more than 3,000 meters, and for the 'ski-bunny' who flounders unsteadily on the arm of her ski instructor, and for whom 'winter sports' mean dancing at the five o'clock social".[35] Accordingly, "the savvy skier wants a fur-lined, hand-stitched waterproof boot equipped with straps for the instep and ankle, and a studded sole. The elegant lady skier, sporting plus fours and a Tyrolean hat, opts for ski boots in white and blue, white and brown, and other such combinations".[36] This marks the construction of unmistakably gendered distinctions: the man as a

[VII] Bally 1938; designer unknown
(Historical Archives of Bally Schuhfabriken AG)

solitary, impassioned, and experienced sportsman; the woman for whom skiing is a merely secondary leisure pursuit, and who sees fashion as her primary concern. A striking aspect is how the ski boot's fashionable elements were often expressed entirely in the details—in the form of a coloured strap, for example. As ever, the focus was directed at creating a serious high-quality boot, although one in which fashionable features helped to make the appearance slightly more relaxed and "accessible" [FIGS. VI, VII].

The Utility Shoe as a Fashionable Consumer Product

While it was possible, as Anne Sudrow has demonstrated, to define the role of the standard shoe in relatively unambiguous terms, the fashion shoe was transformed into "a tool for breaking through old class divisions and a means to achieving multilayered, alternative, and more highly differentiated constructions of identity and social belonging. Standard footwear had historically been viewed as specific to a particular region, nation, or social class, whereas fashion was considered to be cosmopolitan and capable of transcending boundaries".[37] People might show how they belonged to a particular social group by (for example) wearing *golf shoes* or *sports shoes.*

Known as the *Spectator Shoe,* one design signalled through its whiteness (a bold colour choice for men's shoes in this period!) that the wearer did not have to get his feet dirty through work,

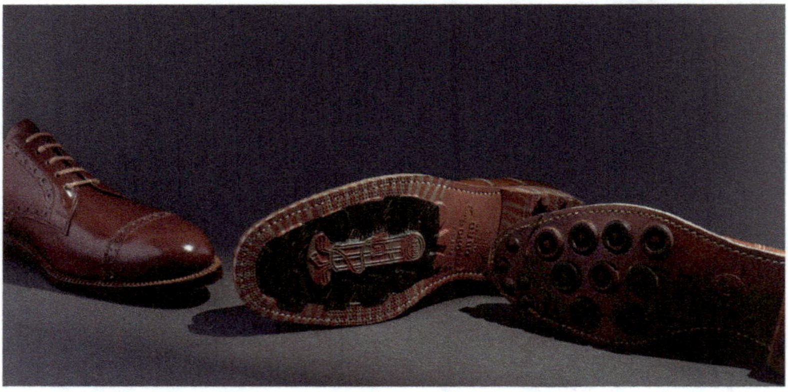

[VIII] Golf shoe soles
(Historical Archives of Bally Schuhfabriken AG; photo: Manuel Fabritz, © Bally)

and that his sporty appearance was a reference to the way he chose to tailor his leisure time. The shoe was practically a symbol of the wearer's cosmopolitan spirit and, of course, a sign of belonging to a more prosperous social class characterized by a sharp sense for design. While the need to emphasize social qualities by means of fashionable dress was initially limited to a relatively small social class, it played an increasingly important role among less wealthy sections of the population as well.[38]

Bally described golf shoes [FIG. VIII] in similar terms to those applied to ski boots:

We draw a distinction between the serious golfer and the amateur lady-golfer, for whom enjoying an aperitif on the club terrace is more important than the game itself. Passionate golfers know that the golf shoe has to be sturdy, strong, and weatherproof. For golf courses in Great Britain and France, where the ground underfoot is often sandy or sparsely covered with grass, the golfer can often make do with footwear on the more fashionable end of the scale. Depending on the terrain, the golfer may opt for rubber or studded leather soles.[39]

A feature in *Das Werk* magazine made the following observations about Swiss sports shoes: "Then there is a category known as *sports loafers*, several models of which have been adapted to serve as practical walking shoes for town, and can also be colour-coordinated with the wearer's outfit."[40] The fashionable

[IX] Bally, sports loafers
(Historical Archives of Bally Schuhfabriken AG; photo: Manuel Fabritz, © Bally)

aspect of these models played a considerably more important role than was the case for pure sports footwear or practical utility shoes, while still offering a high level of protection from the cold and wet [FIG. IX]. Another subcategory was known as the *luxury sports shoe* [FIG. IX], to be worn "while walking the promenade at the spa resort and, if need be, on the golf course"[41]—in this order of priority.

A *sports loafer* can also be frequently spotted on the golf course, a terrain to which its thick, heavily ribbed natural rubber sole is well suited [...] The leather comes in fashionable colors that can be stylishly coordinated with the wearer's clothing. They are donned by gentlemen wearing knickerbocker suits, and can also accessorize the sweater dress or tailored British tweed suit of a lady's sports outfit.[42]

The daring, playful designs of some of the men's sports shoes held in the *Bally* archives from 1930 to 1950 suggest modellers were venturing into uncharted territory and able to give full rein to their imaginations. There were no direct models for them to base their designs on. At the same time, it is also clear that a great deal of skillful craftsmanship and high-quality manufacturing went into these shoes, deviating considerably from the practices of mass production—and adopting an

[x] Bally, sports shoes
(Historical Archives of Bally Schuhfabriken AG; photo: Manuel Fabritz, © Bally)

approach that would be near-impossible to replicate today. In any event, fashion influenced the design of these shoes to what was probably an unprecedented extent. The shoes' penchant for ornate details owed little to the period's avant-garde design trends, which focused on "pure function"—in particular, the degree to which the object's design fitted its purpose. Thus it seems likely that it was sports footwear that paved the way for men to enjoy more colourful and flamboyant shoe fashions. However, my research has been unable to establish for certain whether all these models were indeed produced and released for sale, or whether they were intended more as display models in store windows or as presentation models.

Seen from another perspective, it is interesting to note how elements of practical and technical functionality were transferred to fashion shoes in an extremely aesthetic manner. This is evident, for example, in the diamond-shaped studding on the sole of the shoe shown in the centre, or the quick-release fastener on the shoe to the right of the picture. Thus, practical utility shoes, with their technical details and innovations, in turn lent inspiration to shoe modellers (or designers, as they are known today) for their creations. Nevertheless, it is not always clear whether a design element actually served a functional purpose, or solely as a sign and cultural reference—in other words, was *designed to look functional.* This interplay survives today, or rather, has been intensified to such a considerable degree that the boundary delineating the fashion shoe from the utility one has vanished [FIG. X].

Summary

Practical utility shoes occupy an interesting interface, revealing fundamental questions about the contemporary relationship between design, functionality, and fashion. The relationship effectively maps onto the creative overlap between technical quality, growing demand for fashion, and the economic interests of the shoemaking industry.

For everyday footwear, the shift from boot to shoe—and hence to a process of fashionable individuation and short-lived designs—took place in around 1920. Anne Sudrow has demonstrated that the fundamental transformation was a process that saw an increasing emphasis on fashionable qualities, and less on footwear's actual value in use. In the following years, this process also took place among less prosperous socio-economic groups, as increased industrialization facilitated the reduction of production costs.[43] It helps to understand this change in parallel with the shift in meaning of the term "functionality" over the course of the 20th century. During this period, the concept underwent a marked shift from a purely technical and practical sense to an increasingly semiotic and symbolic one, which in turn became wedded to fashionable considerations. As a result, criteria that had hitherto played a central role in footwear's value (such as durability and reparability) became less important.

By contrast, functional utility shoes remained (at first) largely immune to fashion's influence. The variety of technical demands put on sports shoes in their respective fields led to innovative developments in soles, materials, and types of construction; one such consequence was the rubber sole's breakthrough into the mass market. Shoe production became increasingly industrialized and more scientific. Between 1930 and 1950, however, fashion did eventually come to play a rapidly increasing role in the design of utility shoes, particularly for sports footwear, albeit often solely in the details. The only exception to this was principally work footwear.

These two factors, technology and fashion, led to unprecedented levels of differentiation in the various types of footwear. How much this genuinely responded to the needs of consumers, and how much it served the shoe industry in its primary quest of increasing sales figures, remains an open question. What is known for certain, however, is that the sports shoe played an important role in the process. It provided a space in which designers were able to pursue technical discoveries and experiments in design, while forging a link between technical, practical-oriented footwear and fashion, something which continues to influence us in the present day.

1 There are no general criteria for defining "utility footwear"; here it serves as an umbrella term for footwear in which the design is geared more towards practical value in use and material suitability than for use as a

statement of fashion and/or social communication—hence it applies primarily to work, military, and sports footwear.

2 Breyer 2012, p. 31.

3 Sudrow 2010, p. 65.

4 Ibid., p. 85.

5 Ibid., p. 85.

6 Ibid., p. 96.

7 Ebert 2010, p. 78.

8 Sudrow 2010, p. 151.

9 The Derby (also known as Molière or Gibson) shoe construction: "This refers to a type of shoe in which the laced section is located above the vamp. The lace can be tightened or loosened to optimize the fit to the wearer's individual instep measurement." (Blatter 2001, II-4-4)

10 Double stitching: "This style probably originated in the Alpine countries. [...] From the 17th century, people began using this method for making sturdy, robust footwear." Typical distinguishing features of this method are the two visible seams: The pierced seam (horizontal) joins the leather upper to the insole rib, the double seam (vertical) joins the leather upper to the mid-sole. (Blatter 2001, VI-3-4)

11 This term refers solely to the Swiss army marching boot (Ordonnanzschuh), as opposed to boots worn by officers or footwear worn by the armed forces of other countries.

12 Laubacher/HAM 2007/13 and Historical Archives of Bally Schuhfabriken AG, Stöckli, around 1970.

13 Historical Archives of Bally Schuhfabriken AG, Stöckli, around 1970.

14 (Das) Werk, 1928/15, p. 21.

15 Grenacher and Bernina refer to types of stud arrangement, each of which uses a different type of hobnail (illustrations of which can be found in: Gleitschutz–Caesar bis zur Himalaya-Expedition, Historical Archives of Bally Schuhfabriken AG, around 1950).

16 Historical Archives of Bally Schuhfabriken AG, Gleitschutz—von Cäsar bis zur Himalaya Expedition, author unknown, around 1950, p. 4.

17 Ibid., p. 5.

18 (Das) Werk, 1928/15, p. 21.

19 See Sudrow 2010, p. 68

20 Ebert 2009, p. 47.

21 The first modern ski binding, late 19th century, invented by the skiing pioneer Mathias Zdarsky.

22 Ebert 2009, pp. 77f.

23 Hengartner 1944, pp. 1f.
24 Ibid., p. 2
25 Ibid., p. 2.
26 Ibid., p. 2.
27 Ibid., p. 2.
28 The sole was fastened with twisted nails (screws), a construction style that was used until recently for military footwear.
29 Hengartner, no date, p. 3.
30 Ibid., p. 6.
31 See Ebert 2009, p. 92.
32 Sudrow 2010, p. 151.
33 Historical Archives of Bally Schuhfabriken AG, Bally Sportausstellung, M.P.F., 1935.
34 Hengartner 1944, p. 3.
35 Historical Archives of Bally Schuhfabriken AG, Bally Sportausstellung, M.P.F., 1935.
36 Ibid.
37 Sudrow 2010, p. 395.
38 Ibid., p. 150.
39 Historical Archives of Bally Schuhfabriken AG, Bally Sportausstellung, M.P.F., 1935.
40 (Das) Werk, 1928/15, p. 21.
41 Ibid., p. 24
42 Ibid., p. 24
43 See Sudrow 2010, pp. 61–96.

Enter the Shoe
Design in the Making

Anna-Brigitte Schlittler

Fashion's decree of skirts of daring brevity has brought the foot into new and striking prominence. It cannot hide nor shirk.[1]

From the 1920s onwards, the fashion shoe moved from the fringes to take centre stage in the European and North American shoe industry. For *Bally*, this development triggered a long process of adjustment. As we shall see, the period under examination (1930–1950) witnessed some controversial debates and radical steps. The focus of this chapter is the so-called *Création* department, in which *Bally* invested heavily. Who were the people behind the emergence of this new specialism?[2] What did the profession of shoe design involve? How did the designers work? What knowledge did they bring to the job and what new knowledge did they generate? With whom did they collaborate? How important was fashion in the years immediately before, during, and after the Second World War?

Sources

The study draws on four collections of material:

- The Design Archive, today housed in what was once the packing and dispatch area, with several tens of thousands of objects: women's, men's, and children's shoes, lasts, heels, and trimmings of all descriptions, as well as a number of "non-Bally" shoes from France, Italy, and Switzerland.[3]
- The two in-house magazines, *Mitteilungen der Bally-Schuhfabriken Aktiengesellschaft*[4] (issued by the holding company) and *Arola Hauszeitung* (issued by *Bally's* sales division). The 1930s saw the beginning of a huge rise in internal corporate communication. *Mitteilungen* had been ongoing since 1916 in the form of company announcements, but in late 1940 it was expanded into a true magazine with its own staff of writers, reporting on all the various, far-reaching activities of the company and quite obviously intended

not only for internal consumption. *Mitteilungen* was joined in 1931 by the *Arola Hauszeitung*, published by the sales organization of the same name, which covered sales-related topics.

- The Board Minutes. These are very detailed for the research period and cast a great deal of light on agreements and disagreements among the directors.
- The archive of *Ballyana* the foundation set up to preserve the history of the Bally family and the *Bally* company.[5] This is a separate legal entity from the company's Historical Archives, housed at a different location.

From *Modelleur* to Design Team

No other item of clothing has to cope with as many different and difficult stresses as the shoe—ranging from foot shape, body weight, and individual peculiarities of gait to the varying terrain underfoot. The competing demands of functionality, comfort, and fashion, coupled with the variety and unpredictability of the materials involved, make shoes extremely challenging from the point of view of design and manufacturing technology. The smallest discrepancies or alterations can have a huge influence on the fit, for example.[6] Not least for this reason, the switch to mechanization was not as swift as with other industrial products, and even after the industry had become almost fully mechanized, around the turn of the 20th century,[7] certain sections of the workflow were still very much the domain of the artisan. This was a time when new styles evolved from *within* the production process, not from a drawing board far removed from it; in short, design lay in the hands of the last- and patternmakers.[8] One of the most successful of these was Johann Hospodarsky (1862–1947), who designed the *Hospodarsky Sandal* for *Bally* in 1923. This was one of the company's most popular models, becoming a bestseller, particularly in the USA, where it was marketed as the *Swiss Sandal*, or *Happyland Sandal*. Indeed, 300,000 pairs had been sold by the late 1940s.[9]

In the then largely anonymous world of industrial shoe design, Hospodarsky was an exception, having a number of documents archived under his own name. He also wrote an account of the course of his professional career. After a demanding and exploitative apprenticeship in the Bohemian city of Budějovice (better known by its German name, Budweis), he spent years travelling as a journeyman, followed by further training in Vienna, where he became familiar with the manufacture of women's shoes and learned the basics of last- and patternmaking at specialist cordwainer night classes.[10] It is from this period that a sort of workbook survives,[11] which provides an insight into the craft of shoemaking at the time. Along with anatomical drawings, it includes technical instructions for the construction and sizing of shoes and various basic patterns and prototype designs. Hospodarsky's work came to *Bally's* attention, so *Bally* brought him to Schönenwerd in 1889, where he would remain in charge of production for 40 years.[12] He was responsible for creating new styles and producing design drawings for serial production. Most of his designs were for high-cut shoes, elasticated boots, lace-up and buttoned boots and, for the British and German markets, low-cut women's shoes with elaborate decorative stitching[13] [FIG. I].

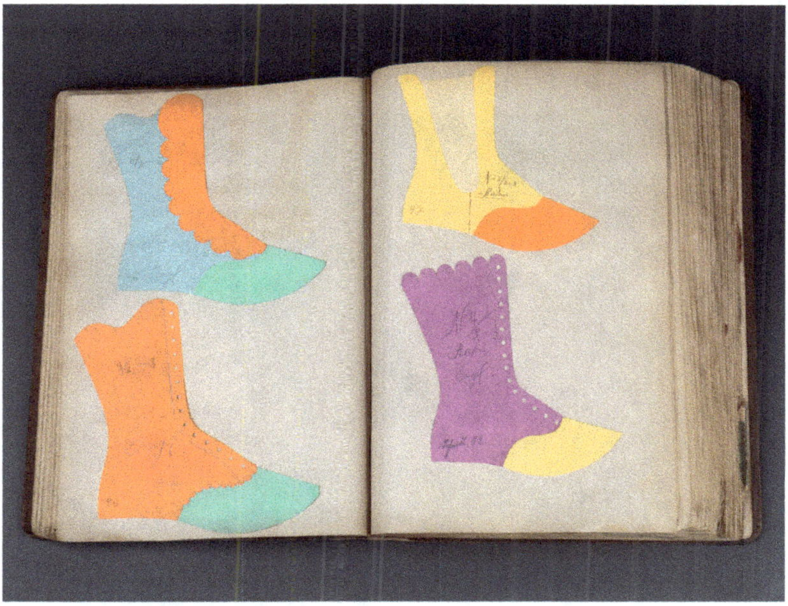

[I] Pattern book
(Historical Archives of Bally Schuhfabriken AG; photo: Manuel Fabritz © Bally)

Bally also has Johann Hospodarsky to thank for the earliest systemization of its shoe designs: each new model was consecutively numbered, and a full-size coloured paper cut-out of the design was pasted into a pattern book.[14] Later, an improved filing system was developed, with a numerical code and shoes arranged in product lines and product families.[15]

According to the company's own internal historiography, there was a radical shift just before the First World War towards "luxury shoes", accompanied by a shift towards the export market.[16] In 1912/13, seven designers and assistant designers with specialist training in shoe design were recruited from Germany and Austria, so that by the summer of 1914 *Bally* had "reached a high point in terms of fashion, promising great prospects for the future".[17] It was not until the following decade, however, that there was any consistent study of fashion or any systematic thought as to how to convert fashion ideas into industrial production processes. In 1929, the company board charged Max Bally with the task of making a "thorough study", whose purpose, amongst other things, was to clarify what exactly the company's "attitude to fashion" should be.[18]

An interest in or even awareness of fashion was by no means shared by all of *Bally's* competitors. Ten years later, at the

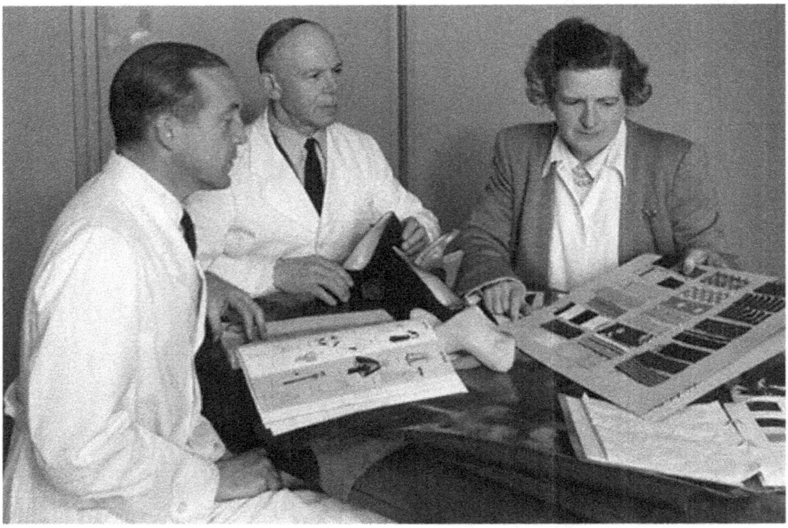

[11] Création (1951)
(Historical Archives of Bally Schuhfabriken AG; © Bally)

1939 Swiss National Expo in Zürich, *Bally's* exhibits were still deemed "bizarre" and dismissed as "gimmickery".[19] But even many shoe manufacturers abroad felt no need to prioritize (fashionable) design. In a paper presented in 1942 to the Royal Society for the Encouragement of Arts, Manufacturers and Commerce,[20] the leather-goods designer John W. Waterer (1892–1977)[21] praised the outstanding skill of the stitchmen still surviving, even in industrial production, but noted at the same time a fundamental neglect of fashion accessories:[22]

There has been too much dabbling with the matter, usually exemplified in the purchase from itinerant vendors of drawings which are, more often than not, entirely altered in character in the factory; or else in leaving the job to the foreman who, excellent workman though he may be, cannot be expected to have or to acquire that intimate knowledge of fashion trends so essential to success. In any event, craftsmanship alone, although an essential attribute of art, is not art itself (although often mistaken for it): without the emotional urge to create, without something to express, even the finest craftsman tends to become little better than a machine. Designing to-day is the expert's job and a whole-time job at that. The designer's job should be to superintend the production of his or her ideas in the factory from their very

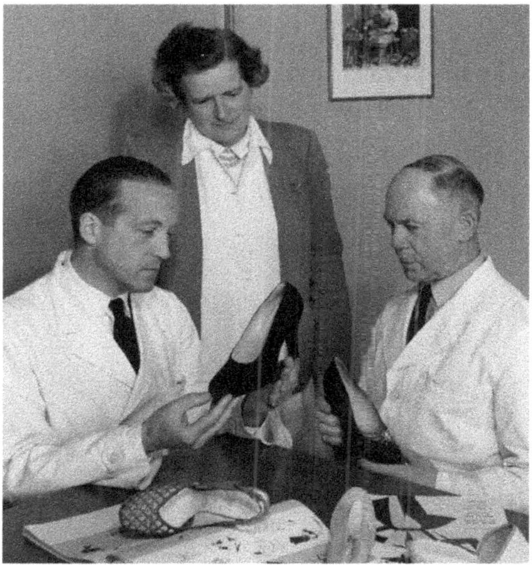

[III] Création (1951)
(Historical Archives of Bally Schuhfabriken AG; © Bally)

inception, and obviously this can only come about if the designer is employed by the producer and is in close touch with all production departments.[23]

At *Bally* in the same period, design—*création,* in the company jargon—was already an "expert's job" [FIGS. II, III].

In the two photographs on the previous pages, the chief protagonists of *Création,* Max Matter, Heidy Studer-Welter, and Albert Eng, are seen posing with the objects which lay at the heart of the new concept of design: not merely shoes and lasts, but fashion magazines, colour charts, and pattern books. The photos date from 1951, the year of the company centenary, but the team had been in their posts as *créateurs* since 1943.

The oldest member of the team—Albert Eng (1888–1966)—had joined the firm as early as 1903, starting in the cutting room but soon moving up to learn about the basic procedures involved in the various stages of fabrication. When *Bally* transformed itself into "a company at the cutting edge of fashion"[24] in the 1930s, he went abroad for further training. Eng provided the interface with production and had the job of "inspiring the lastmaker, evaluating his work from the point of view of both fashion and technology, taking selected models from the design stage to production on the factory floor, from wooden last to leather garment".[25]

Heidy Studer-Welter (1903–1971)[26] had a special role in the male-dominated world of *Création.* As the daughter of one of the caterers at *Bally's* Kosthaus (the resplendent factory canteen building), she was *Bally*-born and bred. She began work in the department in 1942:

> Today Frau Studer represents the "womanly element" in *Création.* Working alongside her male colleagues she is a great asset to the department, bringing her good colour sense and her feminine understanding of special product categories such as evening and summer shoes. With great skill and energy, Frau Studer also oversees the tricky area of fashion shows [...].[27]

Studer-Welter not only designed and organized fashion shows and special press viewings, she was also involved in organizing

Bally's representation at national and international expositions—from Mustermesse Basel to the 1939 National Expo in Zürich and the World Expos in Paris in 1937 and Brussels in 1958.[28] From 1948, she managed Studio Treize, *Bally's* pilot testing lab, and designed shoes for both *Bally Schuhfabriken AG* and its subdivision, *Bally Arola Schuh AG.*[29]

The appointment of Max Matter (1907–1978) as head of *Création* at *Bally* represents a milestone in design history at the company. Fritz Streuli, who until then had been in charge of both sales and *Création,* remained as Matter's superior; *Création* thus technically still fell under sales, but was now granted a higher status of its own (and a greater voice within the company organization).[30] Matter—a nephew of Max Bally—had joined the firm in 1927, working mainly in sales. In 1930 he moved to *Bally-Camsat* in Lyon, where he was employed in the patternmaking department, *Création,* and sales. Returning from occupied France in 1943, he was immediately put in charge of *Création* in Schönenwerd.[31] Matter's encounter with the couturier Robert Piguet was pivotal in the development of the *Création* department. It was essentially thanks to Piguet's influence that *haute couture* became the lodestar for *Bally's* shoe design.[32] By the time he retired in 1972, Matter had become the company's fashion director, as the position was known by then.[33]

The make-up of the first *Création* department also throws light on the company's training and recruitment practices. Since there was no specific professional training for shoe design in Switzerland, the company had a deliberate policy of keeping an eye out for (young) talent.[34] Such talent was nurtured by experienced professionals, like the aforementioned Johann Hospodarsky, who passed on their knowledge by means of in-house "specialist shoe courses". Quite often, however, experienced professionals were simply enticed away from other companies, for example Adolf Streit,[35] and possibly Fritz Kühni, who, having formerly been with the firm Hug,[36] from 1935 to 1965 worked in *Bally's Création* department. In matters of style, moreover, Max Bally, in particular, repeatedly turned to American companies for inspiration in the division of labour and corporate responsibilities.[37]

"Fashion Intermediaries"

In the decades when *Bally* was increasingly evolving into a producer of fashion shoes, fashion itself faced a hostile environment. It was largely excluded from the crucial modernist debates on (industrial) design.[38] When they paid any attention to fashion at all, modernist designers confined themselves, in both theory and practice, to strategies for doing away with it.[39] At best, classic men's shoes were appreciated, by Le Corbusier for example, as "modern object types".[40]

In Switzerland, the Swiss Association of Craftsmen (Schweizerischer Werkbund SWB), founded in 1913, played a leading role in anti-fashion discourse. However, its decidedly unmodish agenda (the "ennobling of industrial work in the interaction of art, industry, and craft through education, raising awareness, and influencing opinion [...]")[41] had little influence on the demand-driven world of industry.[42]

So how did the shoe industry manage the transition from utilitarian products to hedonic goods? In this context, Regina Blaszczyk introduced the useful concept of "fashion intermediaries":

> [B]usiness professionals [...] studied the marketplace, collected data about consumer taste, created products to meet public expectations, and promoted them.[43]

Max Bally (1880–1976), grandson of the firm's founder, was one such fashion intermediary:

> We only have to look at Bally's shoe collection of 50 years ago—something the museum in Schönenwerd allows us to do—and compare it with today's collection. The enormous change that is immediately obvious is the work of Mr Max Bally. Of course, he has had a whole series of creative colleagues working under him, but it was essentially Max Bally who issued the directives that are now being faithfully followed by capable employees. Through extremely hard work, Mr Bally made himself into a world expert on shoes, familiar with the smallest details of the shoe itself, the lasts, the design process, right through to manufacturing and sales.[44]

Max W. Wittstock, director of Arola AG, was probably not greatly exaggerating when he wrote this. From his position on the company board, Max Bally was not only the person mainly responsible for the fashionable orientation of the product range and the steady expansion of the *Création* department,[45] he also built up considerable technical expertise and a far-reaching network of contacts.

Design in the Making

How was the *Création* department itself structured and organized? Who were the main people involved?

There do not seem to have been any organization charts, policy papers, or the like; at any rate, none have survived. All we have is a single document, undated and unsigned, from the bequest of Fritz Streuli, director of *C.F. Bally Schuhfabriken AG*, containing a loose job description. This sets out what "the management of the *Création* department involves: preparing a work programme, collecting and disseminating new stylistic ideas (magazines, acquisition of other producers' designs in the form of drawings and pullovers [prototype sample shoe uppers], criticism and correction of designs, particularly from the point of view of taste".[46]

In the company's internal publications, on the other hand, there are many articles dealing with the design process in the broadest sense:

> Every work springs from an idea. This is particularly true of the manufacture of fashionable footwear. Every new model of shoe is synonymous with a new inspiration. In our case, the workshop where ideas are born is called the the *Création* department.
> If we seek out the *créateurs* in their "studio" with the purpose of learning all sorts of interesting things about their work, the very appearance of the workplace at once gives us a clue that we are dealing here with a highly *artistic* activity. The walls are strewn with sketches and images of every kind, while all sorts of different objects lie on the table: paper patterns, tubes of paint, wooden lasts, shoes, scraps of fabric, leather swatches, fashion magazines, etc. In other words, the artistic endeavour of "creating ideas" has left its mark on the workplace itself.[47]

Another topic often addressed and sometimes described in detail was the interaction between *Création*, sales, and patternmaking. In brief, new designs from *Création* were submitted to the sales teams or the sales manager, who checked the pullovers or last-drawings for technical feasibility and wearability, and signed them off—in other words, approved them for inclusion in the sample collection.[48] The last-drawings or pullovers of the selected models were then handed over to the patternmaking department, where the "modelleurs"[49] would convert them into cutting templates on a special type of last:

> Trustingly, the *créateur* puts it [the design for the shaft, A/N] into our hands, explaining the kernel of his idea, the key element, one might say, of his creation from the fashion point of view. This conversation between the *modelleur* and the *créateur* is necessary and important. It forms the solid connection between sales and patternmaking.[50]

Then came the so-called "*création* of the lasts", adapting or developing the three-dimensional template for production.

A great number of other sources, however, show that this well-ordered process was not always as clear-cut. In the 1930s and 1940s, *création* was an extremely dynamic process that not only produced individual shoes, as described above, but also had to generate a whole new type of knowledge. Changes in fashion had to be constantly detected and monitored in order to transform them into successful styles. In what follows, I give a (non-exhaustive) picture of the resources available to the *Création* department, which in a very short space of time grew to number sixteen people [FIG. IV].

Generating Knowledge[51]

The vital importance of keeping abreast of current fashions and future fashion trends[52] was clear to those in charge at *Bally*, at the latest from the moment when the company committed itself to producing "fashion shoes".

Fashion Reports

It was essential that the *créateurs*, last- and patternmakers, as well as sales staff also had access to current fashion news. From

Jubiläums-Album

Foto No.lo42

Bally-Schuhfabriken AG

Abteilung: Création Schönenwerd

1. S c h e n k e r	Ernst
2. S t i r n e m a n n	Jeannette
3. V o n A r x	Otto
4. W e b e r	Erwin
5. M a t t e r	Max
6. E n g	Albert
7. S t u d e r	Adelheid
8. G u g e l m a n n	Paul
9. L e h m a n n	Robert
lo. L a c k	Peter
11. B u s e r	Walter
12. V o n A r x	Robert
13. P i n i	Peter
14. S t e i n e r	Fritz
15. K ü h n i	Fritz
16. N ü n l i s t	Emil

[IV] Création (1951)
(Historical Archives of Bally Schuhfabriken AG; © Bally)

the mid-1930s, "fashion" was increasingly mentioned in *Mitteilungen*, while from 1932 onwards the *Arola Hauszeitung* ran regular and detailed first-hand reports of current fashions from Paris, London, and New York (years, in fact, before *Annabelle*, the first Swiss fashion magazine, was launched). Particularly detailed reports were provided by Grete Trapp,[53] an experienced fashion journalist and collector who got to attend the Paris fashion shows.

Interest in fashion trends was not restricted to the European and North American centres of fashion. Within twenty years of the end of the First World War, *Bally* had increased its export activities manyfold, so that by 1937 it had a presence on every continent. Thanks to local representatives, information relevant to design and production was now flowing into Schönenwerd from all over the world. For example, from Baghdad:

> In Iraq, the hand-made shoe trade is flourishing. It delivers sandals and light-weight footwear within the shortest timescales and copies imported models with skill and without scruple. What the company Orosdi-Back orders from us, therefore, are those shoes which the local craft industry cannot produce well: largely pumps with very high heels [...] our classic models [...] in many variations, black, brown, blue, gold, and silver, with a variety of different ornaments. Particularly popular are styles with large, striking bows, which are not easy for local shoemakers to copy.[54]

The information gathered in Schönenwerd was not only critical for design and production at Swiss headquarters but was also disseminated within the company "to give a fashion lead to our factories abroad".[55]

Colours

From the second half of the 1920s onwards, not only did the variety of styles increase but *Bally* shoes also became multicoloured: black, brown, and cream were supplemented by a broad spectrum of colours. As early as 1926, Max Bally was arguing for colourful leather uppers and contemplating collaborating with the dye manufacturer Geigy.[56] Besides the complex process of leather dying, precise colour matching was of the utmost importance. An American shoe manufacturer put the problem succinctly in 1921:

> The great difficulty of matching the emerald of the shoe with the emerald of the stocking tends to discourage even the most experienced shoppers. And brilliant shoes that *nearly* match the equally brilliant stockings are taboo in the wardrobes of the well dressed.[57]

Help was at hand with the standardization of the colour palette for the textile and clothing industry, a move which had been in progress for some time. The lead was taken by American organizations such as the Textile Color Card Association (TCCA), founded in 1915, which had already begun to compile seasonal colour charts for the industry during the First World War.[58] These seasonal colour collections were particularly popular with leather-goods manufacturers, whose products now had to match the clothing.[59]

Bally had been in contact with the TCCA, or more specifically its founder and director, Margaret Hayden Rorke, since the 1920s and had been making use of its services for years.[60] The advertising film *Frau Mode spielt auf!* (Lady Fashion Performs!),[61] screened in cinemas in 1939, shows just how aware *Bally* was of the importance of the "correct" colour choice: As long as Lady Fashion can keep playing the colour organ, the shoes produced are in harmony with the customers' overall appearance; if the instrument fails, however, out comes uncouth footwear that causes the mannequins to faint by the dozen.

Museum and Archive

The production of knowledge in the design department was based not only on the knowledge and subsequent material manifestation of current trends, but also on an understanding of the past. The truth of Jakob Tanner's remark that innovation must include a specific mixture of old and new in order to be palatable to the public[62] was borne out at *Bally*, where there was a highly developed awareness that the link between past and present was a necessary foundation for fashion-oriented design. When the museum was opened in 1942 in the "Rock Garden House", it was put under the auspices of the *Création* department.[63]

Housing a huge collection of objects and photographs that aimed to tell the entire world history of footwear,[64] it was no less important as a source of inspiration for designers.

In addition to the museum collection, with its mainly historical scope, the *Création* department also had the Design Archive at its disposal, a repository to which the latest designs were continually being added. (Incidentally, one man played a crucial role in building up both collections: the archivist and conservator Eduard Engensperger, who was curator of the Museum and the Archive until the 1960s.[65] Both collections came to be regarded by *Bally* as sources for corporate historiography since the 1960s at the latest.[66])

Both shoe collections served not only as often intangible "inspiration", but as tangible transmitters of knowledge:

> [W]e must not forget that design knowledge resides in *products* themselves: in the forms and materials and finishes which embody design attributes. Much everyday design work entails the use of precedents or previous exemplars—not because of laziness by the designer but because the exemplars actually contain knowledge of what the product should be.[67]

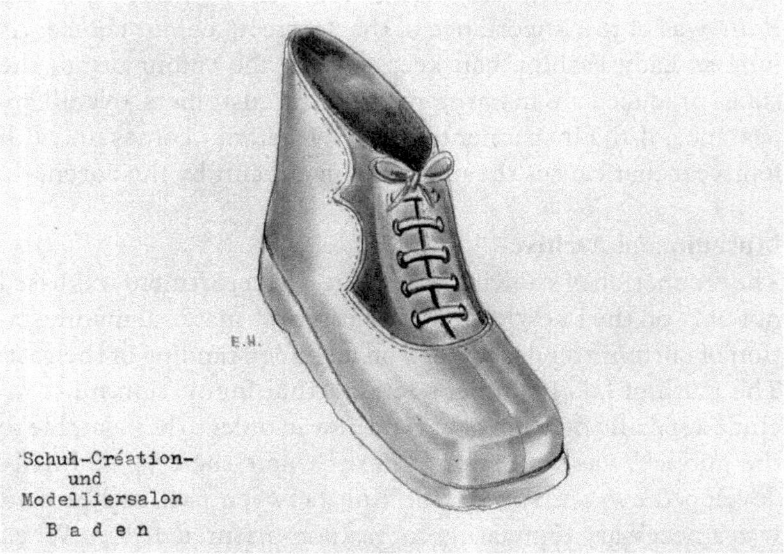

[v] Schuh-Création- und Modelliersalon Baden
(Historical Archives of Bally Schuhfabriken AG; © Bally)

Purchased Design

Despite the emphasis on the independence of the *Création* department, there is numerous and varied evidence of the acquisition of external designs—a practice that was widespread throughout the shoe industry at the time[68] and was also adopted at *Bally,* although to what extent it is hard to say. Various categories can, however, be distinguished [FIG. V].

There are, for example, well over a hundred designs from the Schuh-Création- und Modelliersalon Baden, all of them signed "E.H."[69] and dating from the 1940s. Most are for sturdy, everyday shoes, winter shoes, and house shoes. While Modelliersalon Baden seems to have mainly specialized in so-called "everyday" commodities, *Bally* also purchased intellectual-property rights for designs from famous design studios or design services, including Laboremus in Paris. One of the designers represented by Laboremus was Roger Vivier,[70] whose models *Bally* purchased for its exclusive *Madeleine* collection up until 1939.[71]

Bally not only bought in ready-made models, it also actively sought to collaborate with leading contemporary shoe designers. Most remarkable is its attempt to persuade Salvatore Ferragamo to enter into a "collaborative arrangement". Although Italy's entry into the war meant this plan had to be abandoned,[72] contact was nevertheless evidently maintained: in 1942, Salvatore Ferragamo visited the shoe museum in Schönenwerd; in April 1947, "in a personal letter" he offered "a new patent" and expressed his desire for "a visit by Mr Max Bally in person".[73] Possibly this was in connection with a new wedge heel that was discussed two months later by the board,[74] but it is impossible to determine whether this was indeed the case and whether the discussed heel was ever actually incorporated into a finished model.

The contacts that both *Bally Schuhfabriken AG* and Arola AG sought to establish with Salvatore Ferragamo also shine a light on certain essentially illegal practices that were nevertheless commonplace at the time. During the first visit by the team from *Bally* in 1940, Ferragamo obviously voiced a complaint about the Swiss shoe industry copying his designs. *Bally* retaliated:

[W]e were able, however, to direct his attention to his own compatriots, who were more likely to be involved in such activities, producing imitations which could hardly be told apart from the originals, while, of course, our major ties with the fashion world lie with Paris, London, and New York.[75]

Ferragamo's criticism highlights a problem which remains highly contentious in industrial design to this day: the demarcation between inspiration and copying, or intellectual-property theft. The theft of *haute couture* designs was common practice. In fact, a real "counterfeit couture" existed in Paris,[76] which supplied less well-off clients in Europe and abroad with the latest fashions. Anne Sudrow remarked on something similar in the shoe industry:

The main method employed by shoe companies for acquiring new designs was not developing styles of their own, but copying them. [...] The shoe industry relied on barely concealed design theft, mostly from abroad.[77]

Bally knew how to protect its intellectual property and did so actively. Its advertisements were usually accompanied by the words "designs protected by law", and it vigorously pursued the legal protection of both brand names and styles.

From the 1930s onwards, the firm employed its own lawyer to pursue "violations of the Bally trademark", reported instances of which occurred, for example, in 1931 in Germany, Romania, and Latvia alone.[78] While protection of the brand name was mostly necessary abroad, the protection of designs—pursued with great effort and expense—was mostly directed against competitors at home[79] [FIG. VI]. In the company archives are two huge files of registered designs: Volume III for the years 1939–1945 and Volume V for 1949–1952.[80] They contain collections of photographs, pasted in in date order, often showing just the pullover rather than the finished shoe. These volumes are not only one of the most reliable sources for the dating of individual shoes, but also a visual record of *Bally's* definition of fashion and fashionable footwear over time. The sheer number of designs registered is enormous: In 1939, for example, between

40 and 120 designs, mostly for ladies' shoes, were submitted almost every month to the Federal Office for Industrial Property (Eidgenössisches Amt für gewerbliches Eigenthum)—a total of more than 600 in a single year. The war years that followed saw no drop in output.[81] *Bally* did, however, have misgivings—at least from time to time—about the effectiveness or enforceability of their registrations, owing to "certain considerations" and "corporate friendships".[82]

Studio XIII Haute Botterie. L'avant-garde de la mode pour la chaussure[83]

With its new focus on fashion footwear, *Bally* began to involve "creative clients"—i.e., certain selected retailers, such as Charles Doelker—in compiling its collections.[84] A further step in this direction was the opening of Studio Treize, one of the most interesting and radical attempts to discover what customers wanted through direct contact with the street. When the studio opened at an exclusive address off Zürich's Bahnhofstrasse in 1948, Max W. Wittstock explained that its purpose was to be an "experimental stage" for trying out new types and styles of shoes, colours, and heels. If successful, the ideas could then be applied "more widely".[85]

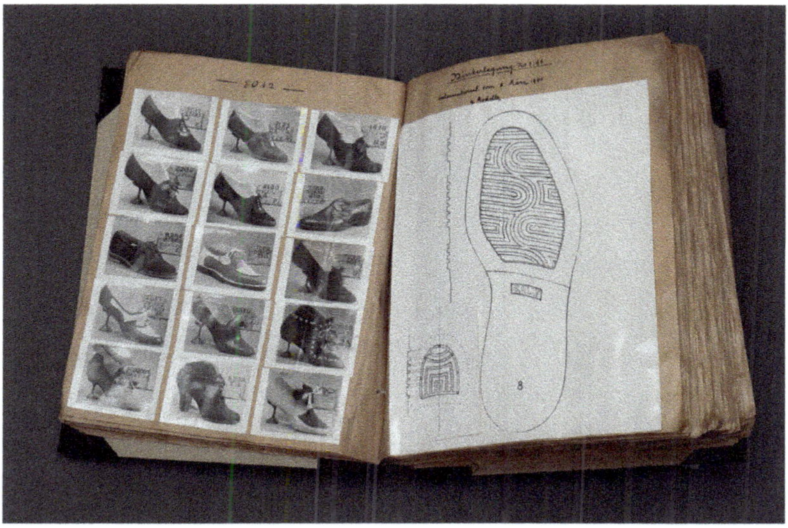

[VI] File of registered designs
(Historical Archives of Bally Schuhfabriken AG; © Bally)

The Zürich studio was probably intended as a sort of prototype; others followed in London, Paris, and New York. Some years later, Max Bally remarked:

Establishing a sample collection with as close to a 100 percent popularity rate as possible can only be done with maximum understanding, not only of clients' requirements, but also, more to the point, of the market situation in the relevant country.
Experience teaches us that it is only through studios that market conditions can be understood, and appropriate decisions reached. [...] Our aim is that these studios, each in its own country, should undertake

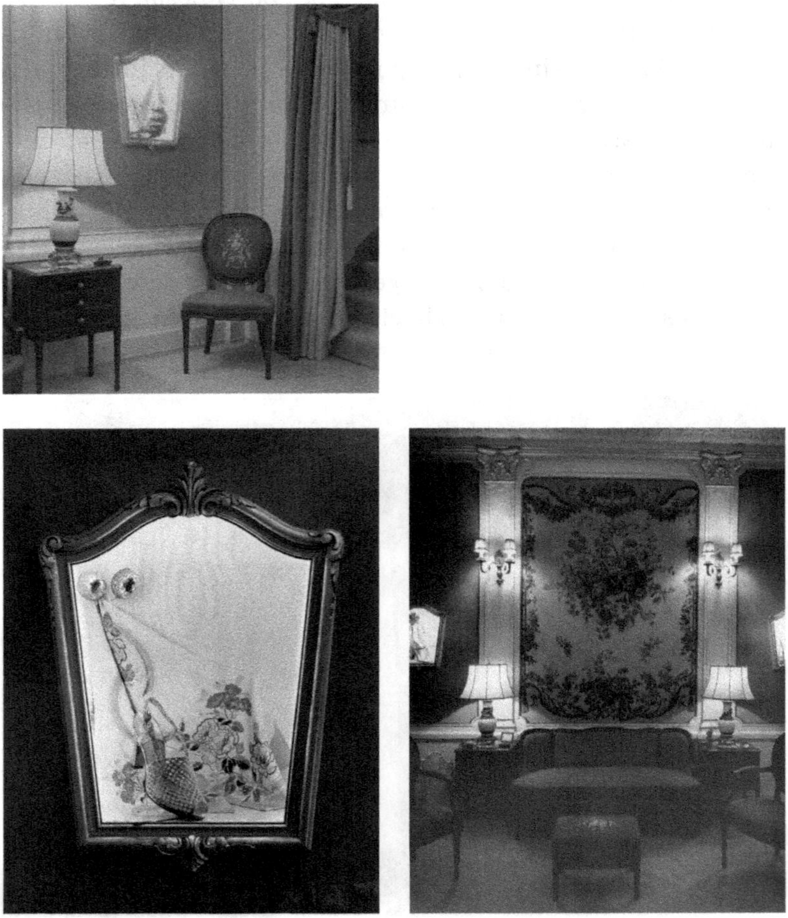

[VII] Studio Treize (c. 1948)
(Historical Archives of Bally Schuhfabriken AG; © Bally)

the sort of product surveys carried out by the sales organization and tell the factory what is wanted[86] [FIG. VII].

The studio was not only a laboratory for creative experimentation, however, but also a place of "haute botterie"—the equivalent, for shoes, of *haute couture*. Accordingly, the shop decor was luxurious. There were no rows of shelves, floor to ceiling, of the sort normally found behind the scenes at ordinary retail premises.[87] Shoes were presented in brightly lit, gold-framed display cases, individually, rather than in pairs, or in ensembles with matching handbags and scarves. Contextualized or, rather, staged in this way, the shoe was "de-commodified", stripped of any mercantile connotations, and turned into a precious object in its own right. With studio decor by the famous costumier and interior designer René Hubert,[88] the parallels with the Paris salons of the postwar era were unmistakeable. Jess Berry describes the way in which the postwar reassertion of traditional gender roles patently expressed itself, not only in the hyper-feminine fashions of Christian Dior, but also in couturiers' salons, where the decor was reminiscent of the aristocratic aesthetic of Louis XVI.[89] From the 1950s onwards, the ateliers that supplied these sales outlets also became increasingly visible to the public, thanks, amongst other things, to magazine articles. According to Berry, this was in order to display and enshrine the artistic and luxurious nature of *haute couture.*[90] Studio Treize imitated the Paris salons in this respect, too: a series of photographs shows Heidy Studer-Welter, who managed the studio on the Bärengasse for several years, at work designing shoes and giving fittings on the studio premises.

Studer-Welter was not the only woman to manage a studio. In fact, Max Bally wanted these exclusive salons to be mainly led by women—in their role as "fashion ladies" (a term he came up with in English):

> Nowadays, these "fashion ladies" are particularly important. In the fashion world, the range of available colours is now near-infinite. At the same time, shoes are technically no longer shoes but simply soles with heels and a few little straps. So the concept of the shoe has to be made interesting by the combination of colours. [...] It is

important to realize that, with shoes, **presentation** is vital. At Bally, we are therefore trying to increase our recruitment of "fashion ladies". Today we already have Frau Studer and Miss Williams working alongside each other. It is important for all our "fashion ladies" to work in close harmony. We need a real exchange of ideas in this area, so that we have **maximum consistency in our product range**.[91]

The role ascribed to women here involves both empowerment and confinement to contemporary stereotypes. The "fashion ladies" were to be barometers in the changing world of fashion and point the way for the collections—and therefore also profit margins. All this was based, however, on the premise that shoes "are technically no longer shoes", but only "soles with heels and a few little straps". In the male-dominated *Création* department, the comparatively important position of the "fashion lady" in the newly formulated design framework was predicated on the feminization of the shoe as an object; in other words, on a focus on the superficial with an implicit disregard of underlying structure and construction.

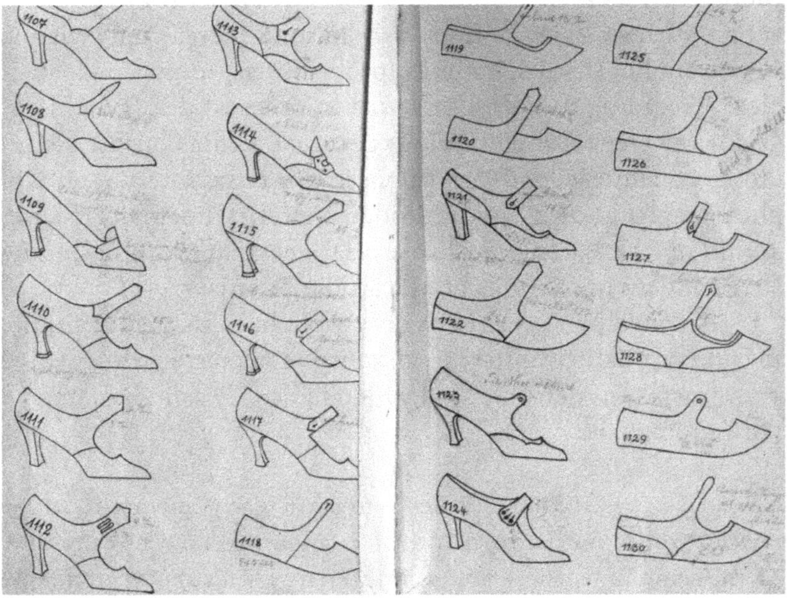

[XIII] Cutting templates (1908)
(Historical Archives of Bally Schuhfabriken AG; © Bally)

The nature, extent, and duration of the influence exercised by the studios on shoe design could not be determined from the sources available. It was probably not without controversy, as an internal document written by Marc Oboussier in 1961 entitled "The Problems of the *Création* Department" suggests. A manager at *Bally* for many years, Oboussier maintained that "the New York studio bore very little fruit, the Zürich studio even less".[92]

Shoe Design—Fashion Design—Industrial Design

Industrialization is generally equated with automation and standardization. This was not entirely true of shoe production, however. At *Bally,* for example, although organized on the principle of division of labour, manufacture was initially entirely done by hand.[93] The first *Singer* sewing machines were installed in Schönenwerd in 1854; the *McKay* stitching machine, a milestone in mass production, was launched in 1868.[94] In the rapidly growing urban centres of Europe, specialist shoe shops had in fact emerged by as early as the second half of the 18th century, selling ready-made shoes in large numbers.

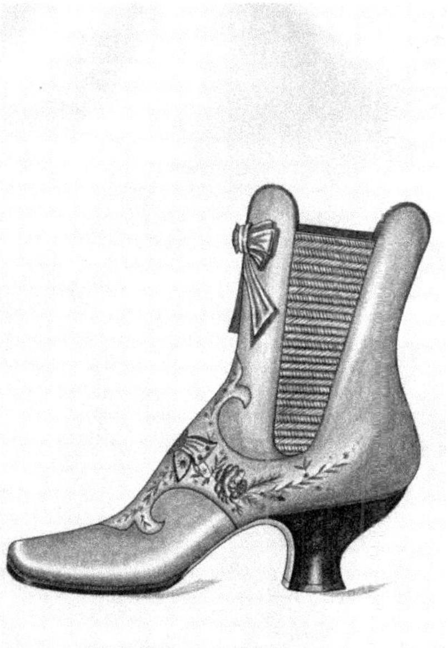

[IX] Shoe design (?) by Johann Hospodarsky (1885)
(Historical Archives of Bally Schuhfabriken AG; © Bally)

Manufacture and sales were therefore no longer conducted under one roof, as they had been in traditional workshops.[95] The anecdote about the company's founder, Carl Franz Bally, bringing back twelve pairs of shoes from Paris for his wife without even knowing her shoe size, illustrates how commonplace ready-made shoe manufacture already was in the mid-19th century.[96] Creative design in industrial conditions—to which little attention has so far been devoted in the literature—remained primarily rooted in the time-honoured repertoire of shoe types whose forms did not change. Variety was created, if at all, through the use of different trimmings. This was as true of men's shoes as of women's.[97] The variations in surface design can be traced in the Design Archive. Shoe styles from the early decades of the 20th century differ from one another

[XA] Fritz Kühni, ideas scrapbook and designs (1930s) (Historical Archives of Bally Schuhfabriken AG; photo: © Ballyana)

mainly in their stitching, appliqué decorations, buckles, etc. In this period, parallels with *les grands bottiers* are evident. One of the best-known of these was Pietro (Pierre) Yantorny (1874–1936), "le bottier le plus cher du monde",[98] who from 1898 onwards supplied a wealthy European and American clientele with shoes of "classic style and artistic design".[99] *Bally's* 1907 appointment of Adolf Streit, an "experienced bottier",[100] trained in Paris, must have been in response to this strongly handcraft-oriented type of design.

By the 1920s, however, it was becoming clear that industrial mass production would soon overtake *les grands bottiers*. "The shoe that answers fashion's call"[101] was a matter for industry, which was far better equipped to transform the shoe from a functional object to a consumer product that followed and reflected changing fashions. The key was standardization, a route already tried and tested by protoindustrial enterprises, which were able to react to the twists and turns of fashion and, ultimately, to pre-empt them and determine their course.[102]

With the new focus on fashion, the requirements of shoe design altered, and, with them, the design profession itself. The shift in the knowledge base was striking: While the *modelleur* drew on a tried-and-tested repertoire, which meant, among other things, understanding and implementing the "knowledge implicit in the object itself",[103] the designer's knowledge base was different and much broader. Ties to the artisanal tradition loosened; the knowledge of producing by hand went into decline. In its place came knowledge of the latest fashions in modern urban centres abroad, trends in colour, style, and materials, and even the preferences and whims of the targeted clientele. The photographs [FIGS. II, III] of Max Matter and his team illustrate the type of resources they drew on: fashion magazines, colour and material charts, fashionable footwear. The *créateurs* were no longer required to master the craft of shoemaking *à fond*. At the same time, their self-perception also changed. *Bally's* internal publications liked to point out the freedom enjoyed by its designers, and the key role played by the "creation of ideas",[104] conjuring up the popular image of the artist's studio with its "walls strewn with sketches and images of every kind".[105] This idea of "artistic freedom" might have been a myth, cultivated within the company and resonating with the contemporary discourse about the role and definition of creative design within industry. Nevertheless, a marked change in attitude is clear from the archives: While Johann Hospodarsky's illustrations are primarily carefully executed technical design drawings and reference anthologies on cuts and form, the sketches by Fritz Kühni (1908–2000), in all their colourful variety, are expressions of a creative *process*, intimately connected with the concept of modern design[106] [FIGS. IX, XA, XB, XC].

At *Bally*, the development of a contemporary concept of design within the industrial context was inseparably linked to fashion. By the late 1920s, the board of directors already believed that fashion was the key to commercial success—even if now and then it bemoaned the antics and vagaries of "fashion, which has an increasing tendency to move in a downwards direction, from hat and dress to shoes, and, once there, to make capricious demands for far too much choice and far too many changes".[107] Its faith in fashion was obviously not ill-founded: In 1934, after a few difficult years in the wake of the global economic crisis, *Bally* was able to increase its production considerably once again

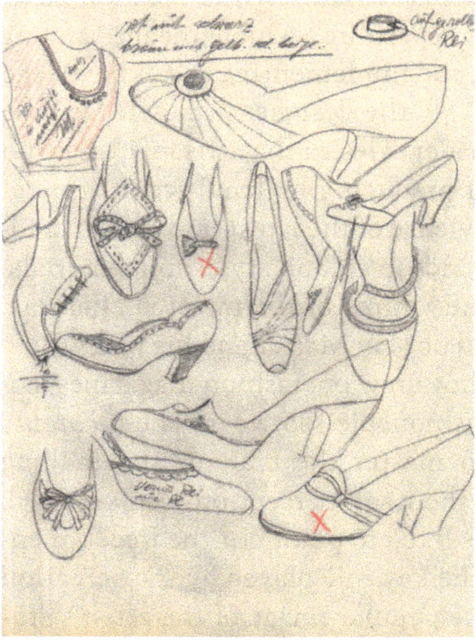

[XB] Fritz Kühni, ideas scrapbook and designs (1930s)
(Historical Archives of Bally Schuhfabriken AG; photo: © Ballyana)

and take on a further 850 workers.[108] This success was mainly ascribed to "contact with the [foreign] capitals of the fashion world".[109]

It is evident that the focus on fashion in the product range also had some negative results. It is true that Max Bally, the most passionate advocate of this new direction on the company board, encountered very little opposition, although there were probably some controversial debates around actual organizational implementation and possible financial risks. Most striking, however, is the practical criticism from the production department. This is where it becomes clear that the greater freedom and sense of independence enjoyed by the design department went hand in hand with a greater distance from the manufacturing process—sometimes with serious consequences. Even small changes in the construction of a shoe, or the introduction, for example, of new materials, could have adverse or even disastrous effects. In the present context there is room only for a few examples of this friction between design and production. In summary, it occurred in essentially three areas. Firstly, new materials presented difficulties, particularly during the war years.

[xc] Fritz Kühni, ideas scrapbook and designs (1930s)
(Historical Archives of Bally Schuhfabriken AG; photo: © Ballyana)

The *Création* department, which was enthusiastically designing shoes made from wood, cork, straw, "ersatz materials", etc., was confronted with a massive increase in the number of shoes being returned for repair: From late 1938 to early 1943 post-sale repair costs more than doubled, as *Bally* had to foot the bill for replacing defective jointed wooden soles, broken reclaimed-rubber soles, *zoccoli* cork soles, and cork wedge soles.[110] Secondly, producing shoes from these types of materials slowed down the normal production process. For example, the employee responsible for overseeing the production of lasts complained that his area's output was falling behind:

> One can see from this what a burden these fashion items are for the machinery. One has to remember that lasts are what make shoe production productive, whereas for each pair of wedges or cork soles produced you are only ever going to get one pair of shoes for sale.[111]

Thirdly, it was sometimes difficult or impossible for the styles demanded by fashion to be satisfactorily implemented by the production department at all. Perhaps unsurprisingly, the high, slender stilettoed heel presented particular problems. At first, *Bally* found that the only way to deal with the unsolved technical difficulties (the heels tended to break off easily) was communication: One tactic was to enclose a note with stiletto-heeled shoes saying that the factory could not accept any liability for broken heels, on the grounds that, "of course, the STILETTO heel is advertised as an adornment for the feet and not as an item for practical use".[112] Another approach was to instruct sales personnel to apply "tact and discretion" in advising "heavy and corpulent customers" and those "who obviously cannot wear this type of shoe with the necessary care and discernment" against ever purchasing them.[113]

"Bally Offers More"[114]

The emergence of product design in the 19th century was not only theoretically underpinned, reflected, and driven by manifestos, programmatic pamphlets, and scientific discoveries; industry itself, with its huge variety of practices and methods, was perhaps the most important protagonist.

Over the decades covered by this research, *Bally* found a way of positioning itself successfully in the increasingly fashion-oriented global market through the growth of its own *Création* department. By developing firm ties to the fashion system, with its specific procedures and knowledge base, *Bally* was able to free itself from the traditional design context and forge ahead with its own decidedly modern and independent style.

1 Vogue, vol. 57, no. 9, 1 May 1921, p. 3.

2 Although Bally also stocked a large and varied selection of men's shoes that were also increasingly obliged to satisfy fashion criteria (see Daniel Späti's essay in this volume, p. 77), I have chosen to concentrate here on women's fashion shoes, which were "Bally's speciality" ("Gedanken zur Entwicklung des Ballyschuhs", 24 November 1969, p. 1; Ballyana, Streuli Bequest M./P-SM/1).

3 It is unclear when and where the Design Archive was founded. According to Alfred Wildi, the display cases with prototypes were already in existence when he started work in Bally's Création department in the mid-1950s. At that time, they were housed in the "Haus zum Magazin" (email from Ursula Gut, 26 August 2019). According to Ursula Gut, who became curator of the museum in 1990 and of the Bally Archives in 2010, all the objects and documents still in existence were moved to their present location in 2009 (conversation with the author on 15 August 2019).

4 Renamed "Mitteilungen der Bally-Schuhfabriken A.-G." in June 1938 and "Mitteilungen der Bally Schuhfabriken AG Schönenwerd an ihr Personal" in January 1942.

5 www.ballyana.ch.

6 Fred J. Klaus recounts a telling anecdote illustrating this very problem, under the title "Die Chaussierprobe", Klaus 1985, pp. 22–24.

7 Riello 2006, p. 233.

8 For a concise description of workflows in the German shoe industry, see Sudrow 2010, p. 169.

9 Mitteilungen, vol. 7, no. 16, 15 July 1947, p. V.

10 Ibid., no. 15, 1 July 1947, p. III.

11 Folio without a shelf mark.

12 Mitteilungen, vol. 7, no. 15, 1 July 1947, p. IV.

13 Ibid., vol. 10, no. 7, 1 March 1950, p. II.

14 Ibid., no. 12, 15 May 1950, p. II.

15 Ibid., p. II.

16 Bally was not only the largest producer of shoes, but at certain times accounted for as much as 95 percent of Switzerland's shoe exports (Mitteilungen, no. 14, 15 April 1937, p. 4).

17 Mitteilungen, vol. 10, no. 7, 1 March 1950, p. III.

18 Board Minutes, 16 August 1929, p. 1.

19 Schweizerische Schuhmacher-Zeitung, vol. 65, no. 12, 15 June 1939, p. 182.

20 Waterer, John W.: "The Industrial Designer and Leather" in: Journal of the Royal Society of Arts, vol. 91, no. 4629 (25 December 1942), pp. 56–72.

21 http://arts.brighton.ac.uk/collections/design-archives/resources/rdis-at-britain-can-make-it,-1946/john-waterer (accessed 29 July 2019).

22 Waterer, John W.: "The Industrial Designer and Leather" in: Journal of the Royal Society of Arts, vol. 91, no. 4629 (25 December 1942), p. 61.

23 Ibid., pp. 62f. This analysis did not just apply to the situation in British industry. See Sudrow 2010, p. 168.

24 Mitteilungen, vol. 3, no. 19, 1 September 1943, p. VIII.

25 Ibid., vol. 13, no. 17, 1 September 1953, p. IX.

26 Her first name is spelled in a variety of ways in the sources: Heidy, Heidi, Adelheid.

27 Mitteilungen, vol. II, no. 9, 1 April 1942, pp. 11f.
This "role assignment" was also common in other industries; see, for example: Buckley, Cheryl: Potters and Paintresses. Women Designers in the Pottery Industry 1870–1955; London 1990.

28 Bally Arola Hauszeitung, vol. 31, no. 89, December 1962, p. 12.
Bally was a very frequent exhibitor at both national and international expos and trade fairs. On its landmark show at the 1939 Swiss National Expo in Zürich, see Katharina Tietze: "'A Fairy-Tale Affair ...!' Bally Shoes at the Swiss National Exposition of 1939", p. 155 in this volume.

29 Ibid., p. 12.

30 Board Minutes no. 437/25.5.1943, p. 2; and no. 443/15 June 1943, p. 1.

31 Mitteilungen, vol. 12, no. 17, 1 September 1952, pp. 1f.

32 Neue Zürcher Zeitung, no. 463, 5 October 1971, p. 33.

33 Mitteilungen, vol. 32, no. 7/8, July/August 1972, p. 6.

34 For example, Othmar Gisi; see Mitteilungen, vol. I, 15 May 1941, p. VI.

35 Ibid., p. VIII.

36 Board Minutes no. 253/28 March 1938.

37 For example, Board Minutes no. 93/24 November 1936, pp. 3f.

38 See Schmelzer-Ziringer, Barbara: Mode Design Theorie; Vienna et al. 2015, pp. 21–36.

39 See Stern, Radu: Against Fashion. Clothing as Art, 1850–1930; Cambridge Mass. 2004; Loos, Adolf: "Damen Mode 1898" in: Gesammelte Schriften; Vienna 2010, pp. 175–181.

40 Breward 2016, p. 187.

41 Quoted in Gnägi, Thomas et al (eds.): Gestaltung Werk Gesellschaft. 100 Jahre Schweizerischer Werkbund SWB; Zürich 2013, p. 53b.

42 Wild 2016, p. 121.

43 Blaszczyk 2008, p. 6.

44 Arola Hauszeitung, vol. 20, no. 58, December 1951, p. 3.

45 See, for example, Board Minutes no. 235/23.12.1937, p. 4.

46 Ballyana, Streuli Bequest, P-SM/1.

47 Mitteilungen, vol. 3, no. 4, 15 January 1943, p. IV.

48 Ibid., vol. 10, no. 6, 15 February 1950, pp. If.

49 The name by which Bally's designers were known.

50 Mitteilungen, vol. 10, no. 6, 15 February 1950, p. II.

51 I am expressly excluding "scientific market research" from this discussion; see Wild 2019, pp. 300–320. A separate study would be needed to investigate the influence of the US shoe and leather industry and its associated organizations. Particularly during the period covered by this study, there was a great deal of travel by all members of the company board.

52 On the history of the study of fashion trends, see Blaszczyk 2018, pp. 1–32.

53 For example, her first article written for the Arola Hauszeitung, no. 4, 1932, pp. 4–11.

54 Mitteilungen, vol. 1, 1 July 1941, p. II.

55 Board Minutes no. 219/24 April 1941, p. 4.

56 Board Minutes, 16 July 1926, p. 2.

57 Blumenthal, F.: Amalgamated Leather Companies; quoted in Blaszczyk 2012, p. 163.

58 Blaszczyk 2012 and 2018.

59 Blaszczyk 2012, p. 166.

60 Mitteilungen, vol. 4, no. 10, 15 April 1944, pp. 1f.; Arola Hauszeitung, vol. 18, no. 52, December 1949, p. 39.

61 On the economic context, see Roman Wild's essay in this volume, p. 21.

62 König 2009, p. 141.

63 When the board discussed financing the purchase of objects for the collection, they concluded by explicitly allocating the costs to the Création department (Board Minutes no. 16/15 June 1936).

64 https://www.aarauinfo.ch/entdecken/bally-schuhmuseum-sch%C3%B6nenwerd (accessed 15 July 2019).

65 Mitteilungen, vol. 2, no. 6, 15 February 1942, p. VII; Mitteilungen, vol. 29, no. 2, February 1969, p. 2.

66 Mitteilungen, vol. 23, no. 4, April 1963, p. 11.

67 Cross 2007, p. 125.

68 For example, after his trip to the USA in 1936, Max Bally noted that most factories purchased sketches or pullovers (Board Minutes no. 93/24 November 1936, p. 4).

69 Loose-leaf folder without shelf mark.

70 Nenno 2016, p. 36.

71 Arola Hauszeitung, vol. 34, no. 98, December 1965, p. 11. For a detailed discussion, see Nenno 2016, pp. 35–46.

72 Arola Hauszeitung, no. 27, June 1940, p. 3. Although Salvatore Ferragamo is not actually named, he can be identified unambiguously from location details, etc.

73 Board Minutes no. 665/3 April 1947, pp. 2f.

74 Board Minutes no. 674/9 June 1947, p. 1.

75 Arola Hauszeitung, no. 27, June 1940, p. 4.

76 Hawes 2015 [1938], p. XX.

77 Sudrow 1910, p. 170.

78 Board Minutes no. 241/15 November 1931.

79 Board Minutes no. 367/24 November 1938, p. 2.

80 Shelf mark 101/14/385-2. The whereabouts of the missing volumes is unknown, as is whether this rate of registration was sustained after 1952. According to oral communication received by phone from the Swiss Patent Office (Eidgenössisches Institut für Geistiges Eigentum) on 15 January 2020, old records have not been digitalized and it would therefore be extremely time-consuming to clarify this question.

81 Numbers of registered designs: 1940: 391; 1941: 692; 1942: 590; 1943: 742; 1944: 305; 1945: 536.

82 Board Minutes no. 367/24 November 1938, pp. 2f.

83 Also: Studio Treize.

84 Oboussier, Marc: "Die Probleme der Kreationsabteilung", p. 2; Ballyana, P-SM/1, Streuli Bequest, p. 2.

85 Arola Hauszeitung, vol. 17, no. 49, December 1948, pp. 33f.

86 Bally, Max: "Eindrücke über die führenden USA Schuhunternehmen anlässlich meiner Herbstreise 1954" (Impressions of Leading US Shoe Companies Gleaned During My Trip of Autumn 1954, addressed to the dele-

gates and directors of the Bally Schuhfabriken AG), pp. 12–14; Ballyana, P-WB/7, Konglomerat 1573.

87 When they redesigned Bally's flagship store in London's New Bond Street, David Chipperfield Architects chose to incorporate a nostalgic evocation of these shelves. See https://davidchipperfield.com/project/bally_london_new_bond_street_flagship (accessed 24 September 2019).

88 Arola Hauszeitung, vol. 28, no. 80, September 1959, p. 39.

89 Berry 2018, pp. 23f.

90 Ibid., p. 24.

91 Bally, Max: Impressions of Leading US Shoe Companies Gleaned During My Trip of Autumn 1954, addressed to the delegates and directors of the Bally Schuhfabriken AG, pp. 12–14; Ballyana, P-WB/7, Konglomerat 1573.

92 Oboussier, Marc: "Die Probleme der Kreationsabteilung", p. 1; Ballyana, P-SM/1, Streuli Bequest.

93 Hundert Jahre Bally-Schuhe, 1951, p. 18.

94 Ibid., p. 28.

95 Riello 2006, pp. 12f.

96 Scalabrin 2009, pp. 109f.

97 Ibid. 2006, p. 77.

98 Bossan 2004, p. 84.

99 Ibid., p. 84.

100 Mitteilungen, vol. I, 15 May 1941, p. VIII.

101 Vogue, vol. 57, no. 9, 1 May 1921, p. 3.

102 Riello 2006, pp. 55f; Styles 1993, pp. 528f.

103 "[...] traditional crafts are based on the knowledge implicit within the object itself of how best to shape, make and use it. This is why craft-made products are usually copied very literally from one example to the next, from one generation to the next" (Cross 2007, p. 125).

104 Mitteilungen, vol. 3, no. 4, 15 Janaury 1943, p. IV.

105 Ibid., p. IV.

106 On the function of the sketch in the production of knowledge and understanding in design, see, for example, Cross 2007, p. 116.

107 Mitteilungen, no. 21, 1 August 1938, p. 2.

108 Ibid., no. 7, 1 January 1934, no page no.

109 Ibid., no. 8, 15 January 1934, no page no.

110 Board Minutes no. 436, 20 May 1943, appendix "Spezialprotokoll".

111 Board Minutes no. 293, 14 June 1938, p. 1.

112 Mitteilungen, vol. XV, no. 21, 1 November 1955, p. V.

113 Ibid., p. VI. The problem was solved by Roger Vivier at about the same time: He designed the "Skyscraper" for Christian Dior and used a type of steel developed by the munitions industry (Semmelhack 2008, p. 50).

114 Advertising slogan from the 1930s.

Real Gold?
A Material for 1930s Shoes[1]

Katharina Tietze

On 24 January 1937, the *Neue Zürcher Zeitung* published an article entitled "Mode in Gold", which reported that:

> Fashion has adopted the gold standard. Now that we've reached the high point of the season, everything is giving way to gold. Gold jewelry is being worn everywhere [...]. Gold sandals have the advantage of matching clothes of any colour. Made of gold leather or moiré and embroidered with gold sequins, they are frequently worn over ultrafine stockings with a golden sheen. As you would expect, in the evening light the effect is simply dazzling.[2]

This essay will explore 1930s shoes for evening wear produced by the Swiss company *Bally*. The firm's archive in Schönenwerd contains an impressive number of elegant evening shoes made of gold leather, and in what follows I will investigate the materials that were used for these shoes. Are they made of leather plated with real gold leaf or gold foil? Could this really have been the fashion during the 1930s—a decade marked, after all, by the fallout of the Great Depression and general belt-tightening? After introducing these products of the 1930s and analyzing their constituent materials, I will draw comparisons with other lustrous materials from the same era and also cast a critical eye at shoe styles, before concluding with a case study that illustrates the importance of cinema on shimmering fashions. I will explore a range of different factors, including technological developments and cultural perceptions, in order to describe the significance of a specific lustrous material during the interwar period, looking at both its real and metaphorical value.

Bally Shoes

The sheer diversity in the range of shoe models produced during the 1930s is unique in the history of the company. In Schönenwerd, roughly an hour's train ride from Zürich, *Bally* manufactured shoes for women, men, and children ranging from army boots to sports and comfortable footwear. *Bally* shoes were renowned for their quality, with first-class materials worked to exceptionally high standards, generally in classic styles. It is only since the turn of the 21st century that the firm has come to see itself as a luxury brand.

Over a third of the 600 women's shoes dating from the 1930s are evening shoes, and gold leather was used in around half of these (some 120 shoes). Twenty-five of these models are made entirely of gold leather, while a further 84 are decorated with gold leather details [FIG. I]. The gold evening shoes, with heels measuring between six and ten centimetres, are generally closed at the heel or the toe. Open sandals and closed pumps are relatively rare. The photograph shows the characteristic features of *Bally* shoes: Although their shapes and the original lasts are very similar, there is a huge array of decorative elements to go with them [FIG. II]. The gold leather shows some variation; still, the majority of the shoes (which are now almost 80 years old) feature strikingly high-quality uppers. This can be seen particularly clearly here thanks to the use of smooth and textured gold

[I] Bally gold leather evening shoes from the 1930s
(Historical Archives of Bally Schuhfabriken AG; photo: Manuel Fabritz, © Bally)

leather on the heel [FIG. III]. Where gold leather is used as a decorative detail, it is usually set contrasting against another material—generally a fabric, such as green or burgundy satin, in a manner typical of 1930s fashion [FIGS. IV, V]. The combination of gold with black leather or suede is very common, and gold and silver leathers are often used for decorative elements such as ruching or straps.

The shoes in the archives are prototypes which have never been worn. Nonetheless, they force us to wonder what kinds of occasions they were intended for—presumably balls or other dances. They probably provide good support to the foot, and it is easy to imagine how they might glitter and flash when worn under a long evening gown in a festively lit ballroom.

Another reason for the large number of gold shoes in the archives is that many of these models were exhibits in the Swiss National Expo of 1939.[3] Archive and museum coordinator Rebekka Gerber was able to identify more than half the shoes displayed in one case (including the model shown in FIG. VI). During the 1930s, *Bally's* Swiss catalogue listed only shoes with gilded appliquéd *details*. Evening shoes with vamps and sling-

[II] Selection of Bally evening shoes from the 1930s
(Historical Archives of Bally Schuhfabriken AG; photo: Manuel Fabritz, © Bally)

backs made *entirely* from gold leather are completely absent, which suggests that these models were primarily intended for export.

Leather, Gold, Gold Leather

Gold leather unites two different materials: leather is the primary material and serves as a base, while gold provides a finish, a colour, or a coating. The combination of the two materials has its own unique qualities and significance.

Shoes have long been made from leather, with the material lending these objects their unique character. It forms a second (animal) skin that provides a sculptural enclosure for the foot and also displays the marks of its use. The leather is responsible for the typical characteristics of shoes—in particular, the impression they create of the foot or feet—so that, unlike clothes, they retain the shape of the wearer's body even when unworn. They also display signs of wear that vary from customer to customer and which are even, to a point, cherished as such. Thus shoes can also be an artistic medium; they stand not only for the social background of the wearer, but also for their personal biography, as Monika Wagner demonstrates in her examination of

[III] Bally shoe, 1937
(Historical Archives of Bally Schuhfabriken AG; photo: Manuel Fabritz, © Bally)

an installation by Peter Greenaway.[4] Leather also has functional qualities, being capable of stretching, contracting, and absorbing moisture—all of which are indispensable attributes for footwear. *Bally* evening shoes were made using top-quality chrome-tanned kid leather, which is derived from the skins of young goats and is soft, supple, and hardwearing. *Bally* bought its leather from the Heyl'sche Lederwerke in Worms, among other suppliers, and also operated two of its own tanneries in South America.

Gold is a chemical element and the most precious of all metals. It tends to appear at the top of ranking systems for materials.[5] Gold is both an ornament and a means of payment. Its luxurious warm glow symbolizes wealth and power. Gold cannot be manufactured by artificial means, and the rarity of its occurrence is also what makes it so valuable. Of the approximately 100,000 metric tons of gold that exist on Earth, one third is stored by central banks in the form of gold reserves.[6] Because it is a very soft metal, gold objects (including decorative items) are always made of alloys, which may contain silver, copper, palladium, or nickel. Brass and bronze are the most important gold-*coloured* alloys. Brass is an alloy of copper and zinc, while bronze consists of copper and tin. These alloys play a special role when it comes to jewellery. As Eva Heller explains regarding one such brass:

> "Talmi gold", seen today as the epitome of fake or cheap jewellery, derives its name from the Parisian metalsmith Paul Tallois of Tallois & Mayence, whose imitation gold, "Tallois-demi-or", was abbreviated to *talmi*. This alloy of copper and zinc can even contain up to 1% gold.[7]

The boundary between the real and the fake is thus often fluid. Rather than being cast in solid gold or gold alloy, objects are often merely gold-plated—either through galvanization or using gold leaf, depending on the material in question. A single gram of gold yields around half a square metre of gold leaf.

Gold leather is always made of real leather, but not necessarily of real gold. An example of the latter is an Egyptian sandal held in the collection of the Victoria & Albert Museum. Made around the turn of the Common Era, the leather sole of this shoe is decorated with gold-leaf patterning. There is also a long tradition of manufacturing gold leather for use in wall coverings and bookbindings. Andreas Schulze describes in detail the production process behind the gold leather wall coverings in Schloss Moritzburg, Saxony, which date to around 1725.[8] Here, silver leaf was glued onto the leather before the gold colour was applied using special varnishes. The leather was then decorated with embossing and punchwork and also painted. This is a complex piece of craftmanship, with many stages to the process.[9] By contrast, the 1930s shoes here focused on are industrial products, so the gold coating must have been applied in serial production.

But what are the golden uppers of these shoes made of? The 1936 *Handbuch der Gerbereichemie und Lederfabrikation* (Manual on tanning chemistry and leather manufacture) states that:

> Gold- or silver-plating of high-quality leather involves the use of real gold or silver leaf. [...] With cheap leathers, the genuine metal leaf is generally replaced with artificial bronze powder. Aluminum powder offers a substitute for silver, while gold-bronze consists of a powdered

[IV] Bally evening shoes with gold leather details
(Historical Archives of Bally Schuhfabriken AG; photo: Manuel Fabritz, © Bally)

copper alloy. The binding agent for the bronze is a colourless collodion varnish, which [...] was diluted in order to facilitate spraying.[10]

A 1955 edition of the same guide adds that "sometimes the uppers of luxury women's shoes are made of leather plated with real metal, but sometimes they are made of cheaper imitations".[11]

It is easy to establish the exact materials that were used with the help of an electron microscope; however, this requires a piece of leather for analysis, and naturally the historical shoes in the collection may not be damaged—not even to remove just a few square millimetres of material.

Fortunately, the *Bally* Historical Archives also hold a suitcase containing a description of the shoe manufacturing process, as well as a number of leather samples. The table of contents is dated 16 February 1943. The gold leather, listed as No. 6 in the section on leather used in uppers, is documented as follows: "kidskin, goat, specially tanned or chrome-tanned, decorative and luxury leather." I was able to submit a piece of this leather sample to the Forschungsinstitut für Leder und Kunststoffbahnen, an independent research institute in Freiberg, for

[v] Bally evening shoes with gold leather details
(Historical Archives of Bally Schuhfabriken AG; photo: Manuel Fabritz, © Bally)

analysis. When the electron beam was set to 10 kV, X-ray microanalysis indicated a mass fraction of gold (Au) of 87.1, along with smaller quantities of silver (Ag), carbon (C), and oxygen (O). At an energy level of 30 kV, the beam penetrated deeper into the material and revealed greater mass fractions of carbon and oxygen, indicative of the organic compounds in the leather. This demonstrates that the shoes were made with real gold—a fact that explains the warm glow of the leather, which still looks almost new (after all, gold never tarnishes) and possibly also my lasting fascination with these almost 80-year-old shoes.

How was the gold applied to the leather, and where did *Bally* get its gold leather from? Werner Deutschmann, an employee at *Bally* from 1961 until 1990, went to work at the Emil Waeldin leather factory in Lahr in the Black Forest after completing his apprenticeship as a leather technician at the aforementioned institute in Freiberg. Emil Waeldin was a producer of gold leather, and Deutschmann provides us with the following account:

> Nobody was allowed inside the room. That was where the gold leaf was stored in piles. Around fifteen to twenty women worked in that department. The company was wound up in the early 1970s. Bally was one of its customers, a very demanding customer. I think the factory belonged to the Heyl'sche Lederwerke.[12]

In an interview with Alberta Fabian, a former worker at the Heyl'sche Lederwerke, the journalist Ulrike Schäfer gives a more detailed description of the process:

> From 1950 onwards, the [...] eighteen-year-old worked at Heyl Liebenau in Neuhausen, where she applied gold and silver[13] leaf to finished pieces of leather inside a draft-free room. "It was very delicate work," she explains. "We would take a twelve-centimetre square of wire mesh in a wooden frame and lay it over the gold leaf. Then we would blow gently on it, drawing the fine material onto the mesh and making it stick in place. After that, we would press it carefully onto the kid leather, which had already been coated in a layer of adhesive. We had to take great care to ensure that the gold leaf lined up exactly with the neighbouring piece [...]." Fabian never saw how the gold- and sil-

ver-plated leather—named *Fafnerkid* and *Fasoltkid*, respectively, after the giants [Fafner and Fasolt] from the Germanic *Nibelungen* saga—was subsequently processed.[14]

Golden Shoes

Even in the 1890s, during the earliest days of industrial production, we see shoes made from gilded leather, such as a pair from around 1891 held in the collection of the Metropolitan Museum of Art in New York. The high quality of the gleaming golden uppers on these shoes is readily apparent. The earliest gold shoes in the *Bally* Historical Archives date to 1920. These are a pair of pumps made from a gold leather that has a softer, more muted glow. There are even examples of men's shoes from the 1920s made of gold leather. The shoe collection of the Northampton Museum and Art Gallery in England features lace-up ankle boots with uppers made entirely of gold leather, which were manufactured by Mounts Shoe Factory Co. Ltd. in 1922. Another unusual example is provided by the men's shoes from around 1922 in the collection of the Victoria & Albert Museum, which are made from turquoise marbled leather with gilded leather appliqués. Nonetheless, gold shoes only began appearing in significant quantities during the 1930s. As elegant women's shoes, they constitute a typical item of evening wear during that period—a fact demonstrated by both the article quoted at the beginning of this essay and the numerous shoes held in the *Bally* archives. Golden shoes have come into fashion repeatedly over the years, with the latest incarnation of this being the current trend for golden sneakers and golden Birkenstock sandals. The example of contemporary fashion in the exhibition *The Gold Standard: Glittering Footwear from around the Globe* (on display at the Bata Shoe Museum in Toronto, 2019) is a pair of golden sneakers created by Jeremy Scott for Adidas. Scott's design features a wing motif evocative of the messenger god Hermes. The exhibition also includes a number of *Bally* shoes.

The stylistic elements of the shoes in the collection provide us with information about the significance of gold leather as a material during the 1930s. Two examples from the *Bally* Historical Archives feature classical motifs: an evening sandal with straps of gold leather decorated with a stitched Greek key pattern [FIG. VI], and another golden sandal decorated with a sculptural scallop-shell design reminiscent of the *Birth of Venus*, Botticelli's seminal image of the Roman goddess of love and beauty [FIG. VII].

Golden shoes made by other manufacturers display influences from foreign cultures. One of the most important shoe designers at this time was Salvatore Ferragamo (1898–1960), whose pyramid-heeled shoe [FIG. VIII] refers to a discovery that certainly played a role in gold's rise to fashion: In 1922, Egyptologist Howard Carter presented to the world the treasures from the tomb of Tutankhamun. Many of Tutankhamun's grave goods are made from gold-plated wood, but some (including the iconic mask) are pure gold. Other designs by Ferragamo feature raised toes and wedge soles combined with gold leather, drawing on Eastern influences.

These diverse gold leather shoes adopt motifs from other cultures, while their stylistic features and use of materials allow us to class them as Neoclassical or Art Deco.

[VI] Bally shoe, 1937
(Historical Archives of Bally Schuhfabriken AG; photo: Manuel Fabritz, © Bally)

Innovations in Materials

As shown in the opening quotation from the *Neue Zürcher Zeitung*, not just gold leather, but a wide range of lustrous materials became fashionable in the 1930s. Some of these were natural fibres, such as silk. One typical material used in 1930s fashion was flowing silk satin, which would be cut on the bias to make garments with an especially close fit to cling to the wearer's body. Yet early cellulose-based synthetic fibres were also used during this period. The initial aim with synthetic fibres was to imitate natural materials, so these new fabrics were given names such as "artificial silk". The newly developed fabrics were made by dissolving and regenerating cellulose fibres. Company names such as Vereinigte Glanzstoff-Fabriken AG (United High-Gloss Fabric Manufacturers) show that the lustrous quality of these new materials was considered their defining feature. This particular company was originally founded in 1891 in Oberbruch bei Aachen as a light bulb manufacturer, since at that time light bulb filaments were made from synthetic fibres. However, the founders Fremery and Urban quickly switched focus to textile fibres and began to manufacture

[VII] Bally shoe, 1939
(Historical Archives of Bally Schuhfabriken AG; photo: Manuel Fabritz, © Bally)

cuprammonium rayon, or cupro. This was primarily intended for decorative items such as ribbons and ruching, as it was not yet fine or tough enough to be used for other purposes.[15] The viscose process was developed in England at around this time, and the Glanzstoff-Fabriken switched to this method in 1916, leaving the production of cupro to Bemberg AG, a manufacturer of women's lingerie and stockings.

Another example of a highly fashionable innovation in lustrous fabrics was lamé—a plain-woven material mainly used for evening wear that was made by adding flat metal threads to the warp or weft of the fabric. The 1940 *ABC der Kunstseiden und Zellwollen* (a guide on artificial silks and rayon fibres) states that "thin metallic threads laminated to cellophane are particularly well suited for producing lamé effects".[16] The same reference book describes cellophane *(Zellglas)* as "a generic name for transparent films produced through the viscose, cuprammonium, or cellulose acetate processes". Then there is Lurex, which was invented by a British company and only came onto the market in 1946. Much like today, scientific and commercial innovation inspired and spurred design. Entirely new possibilities were offered by the development of nylon and Perlon,

[VIII] Salvatore Ferragamo, 1930
(Courtesy of the Museo Salvatore Ferragamo, Florence)

the first fully synthetic fibres. Nylon was first launched by DuPont at the 1939 New York World's Fair and revolutionized the stocking industry, along with many other sectors.

These new synthetic fibres were also used in shoes. In one of his sandals, Ferragamo combined gold and silver leathers with a Bakelite heel [FIG. IX]. After the start of the Second World War, *Bally* had to begin using new materials in place of leather. Examples of this include heels coated in celluloid and embossed with a lizard-skin pattern.[17]

Why did lustrous materials come into fashion during the period between the stock market crash of 1929 and the start of the Second World War in 1939? One reason was simply that technical innovations made the manufacture of these new fabrics possible. Another was that shiny materials remained desirable as an expression of wealth and prestige. In Irmgard Keun's novel *The Artificial Silk Girl,* first published in German in 1932 as *Das kunstseidene Mädchen,* the main character expresses her desire to rise through the ranks of society: "I want to shine. I want to be at the top. [...] With everyone respecting me because I shine."[18] This yearning for glitz and glitter offered an alternative to an everyday existence dominated by the economic crisis.

[IX] Salvatore Ferragamo, 1939
(Courtesy of the Museo Salvatore Ferragamo, Florence)

Gold and Wealth in Cinema

Alongside photographs in fashion magazines such as *Vogue*, the film industry (especially Hollywood) also played an important role in the spread of glamorous fashions. Although still mostly shot in black and white,[19] the movie—in essence a medium of projected light and light effects—helped propagate the use of eye-catching materials. When operating on a spectrum between black and white, it is important to enhance the white elements as much as possible. This is done with the help of high-gloss surfaces, which become even more prominent when in motion.

The movie *Gold Diggers of 1933* brings together gold, money, and fashion, with gold serving as both currency and ornament. The word "gold-digger" began to be used as early as the 1910s as a pejorative term for women whose romantic interests are motivated by a desire for money. The musical film, directed by Mervin LeRoy, was based on a 1919 stage play,[20] with the dance scenes choreographed by Busby Berkeley. During the musical number in the opening scene, a chorus line of women dressed in costumes made of coins perform before a backdrop of enormous coins, while Ginger Rogers sings "We're in the Money". At first, the dancers' faces are hidden behind imitation dollar coins which themselves feature a portrait of a woman: the Liberty Head. These may have been based on the Eagle, a gold coin worth ten dollars that remained in circulation until 1933, although the silver Peace Dollar may also have been used as a model. With a black-and-white film, it is hard to tell whether we are looking at silver or gold—but as the song says: "With silver you can turn your dreams to gold." An interlude of dancing is then followed by a kind of fashion show in which young women step through a glittering curtain adorned with a dollar sign, wearing various dresses made of high-gloss fabrics and decorated with coin motifs.

Here, the young women are not only dressed in gold coins—they transform themselves into currency, or are implied to do so. As they do so, the characters in the movie dream of finally getting rich. The motif of dancers dressed in gold coins has historical precedent in the belly dancers of the Algerian Ouled Naïl tribe, who decorated themselves with coins as proof of the wealth they had acquired through their dancing.[21] These performers were very widely known around 1910 and may even have inspired the musical number in *Gold Diggers of 1933*.

As this movie shows, not only was gold valuable, but it was also very clearly associated with currency. This is demonstrated further by the gold standard, a system in which each country's money supply was linked to the quantity of gold it possessed, with the goal of stabilizing currencies and facilitating foreign exchange. The year 1929 nonetheless saw the start of the Great Depression, after which countries gradually began to abandon the gold standard, with the USA among the earliest to do so, in 1933. It was in this year that *Gold Diggers of 1933* was released, and its opening scene embodies a desire for money.

The trend for gold was not limited to the colour, but included gold coins too. "Antique gold jewellery from all eras—the bigger the better—and enormous coins [...] meet the demand for decorative effect,"[22] wrote one correspondent for the *Neue Zürcher Zeitung* in 1937.

A variety of additional circumstances helped usher gold leather shoes into fashion during the 1930s. New technologies enabled the processing of real gold leaf, while new cellulose-based plastics made it possible to give even mass-market products a glamorous sheen. The economic pressures of the time meant that gold also became important in terms of its economic value, while influences from other cultures, such as Egypt, played a role too. As a visual effect and a symbol of glamour, glitter and gloss were a byproduct of photography and especially of motion pictures, where a superficial sheen represented a value that was absent from everyday life. Last but not least, however, there was also a very practical reason for wearing gold evening shoes: "Gold sandals have the advantage of matching clothes of any colour."[23]

1 An earlier version of this text was published under the title "Schein und Wert. Goldleder als Material für Abendschuhe in den 1930er Jahren" in: Martin Scholz, Friedrich Weltzien (eds.): Die Sprachen des Materials. Narrative – Theorien – Strategien; Berlin 2016.

2 "Die Mode schliesst sich dem bewährten 'Ideal Gold' an. Auf dem Gipfelpunkt der Saison angelangt, tritt alles hinter Gold zurück. Überall wird

Goldschmuck zugezogen [...]. Goldene Sandalen haben den Vorzug zu jeder Kleiderfarbe getragen werden zu können. Sie werden vielfach aus Goldleder oder goldfarbenem Moiré, mit goldenen Pailletten bestickt, über hochfeinen, goldschimmernden Strümpfen getragen. Die abendliche Wirkung ist natürlich ausgezeichnet."

3 See Tietze: "A Fairy-Tale Affair…!" in this volume, p. 155.

4 Wagner 2001, pp. 84–87.

5 Rübel/Wagner/Wolff 2005, p. 35.

6 materialachiv.ch (accessed 11.11.2019).

7 Heller 1989, p. 192.

8 Schulze 2011.

9 A modern version designed by Peter Behrens in 1902 for the arts and crafts exhibition in Turin can be found at the Museum für Kunst und Gewerbe in Hamburg.

10 Grassmann et al. 1936, pp. 251–252.

11 Ibid., p. 134.

12 Interview of the author with Mr. Deutschmann, 28 November 2018.

13 This would presumably have been aluminum.

14 Schäfer 2019. With thanks to Rosita Nenno for pointing out this reference.

15 Bauer 1958, p. 48.

16 Arends 1940, p. 196.

17 F.S. 1941, p.1.

18 "Ich will so ein Glanz werden, der oben ist. […] Und die Leute achten mich hoch, weil ich ein Glanz bin"; Keun 2004, p. 45.

19 The earliest Technicolor movies included titles such as The Wizard of Oz and Gone with the Wind, both released in 1939.

20 There had already been a Gold Diggers film in 1929, and the series was continued in 1935, 1937, and 1938.

21 With thanks to Rolf Sachsse for pointing out this reference. See also his captions in LVR-LandesMuseum Bonn: 1914. Welt in Farbe. Farbfotografie vor dem Krieg; Ostfildern 2013, p. 131.

22 "Antiker Goldschmuck aus allen Epochen, je umfangreicher desto begehrter, riesige Münzen […] erfüllen die Anforderungen an dekorative Wirkungen"; Neue Zürcher Zeitung, 25 January 1937, p. 8.

23 Ibid.

Notes on Window Dressing as a New Means of Communication

Henriette-Friederike Herm

Ever since the first department store opened its doors—and windows—in the latter half of the 19th century, generations of art historians and sociologists have engaged in a theoretical debate surrounding the cultural and social significance of consumer goods and their display.

Georg Simmel describes the "shop-window quality of things"[1] as a three-dimensional still life:

> The exhibition, with its emphasis on amusement, attempts a new synthesis between the principles of external stimulus and the practical functions of objects, and thereby takes this aesthetic superadditum to its highest level. The banal attempt to put things in their best light, as in the cries of the street trader, is transformed in the interesting attempt to confer a new aesthetic significance from displaying objects together [...].[2]

Previously, a shop window's main purpose had been to let in light, its initial display function essentially akin to a noticeboard providing information, including on the identity and status of the retailer. But in the 1890s, partly due to electric lighting, shop windows started attracting attention as an advertising medium for the products inside.[3] Associations were forged between the product and certain ideas, values, and perceptions; and communicating an emotional experience with the product became more important.[4] The shop window offered a new interface for communication between the retailer and the customer. As a realm of temptation between the street outside and the shop interior, its purpose was to arouse curiosity and entice people to step inside.

This essay explores the dramatological and curatorial function of window dressing. By drawing on findings from sources uncovered in the *Bally* Historical Archives in Schönenwerd and articles in the *Arola Hauszeitung,*[5] it reveals how in the period 1930 to 1950 *Bally* specifically deployed this new means of communication as a channel by which to visually depict the "philosophy" of the *Bally* brand, thus making the shop window a tool of corporate identity. A critical turning point in this development was the foundation of the retail division Arola Schuh

[I, II] Schuhhaus Modern, Zürich
(Arola Hauszeitung, no. 6, 1932, p. 37)

AG in 1926. The *Bally* company thus had control over the entire process, from design and production to direct retail channels through *Bally-Schuhverkauf AG* (Basvag) and Arola, and indirect retail channels through department stores. The *Arola Hauszeitung* shows the shop window as a creative visual arena, the value of which went beyond the mere showcasing of stock to a space for advertising, sales arguments, and brand identity. This essay traces important actors, presentation motifs, and strategies for the development and fine-tuning of window dressing at *Bally*.

The shop windows were decorated by different people from different sections of the company chain. Well into the 1930s, the managers of the respective stores were the primary decision-makers behind window-display designs. They decorated their shop windows either with materials completely of their own choosing or by incorporating posters and other advertising material supplied with each new season by *Bally-Schuhverkauf AG*, along with a letter giving advice on presentation and sales. This circular, or rather "info pack", contained sheets that could be inserted into frames and that bore images intended to create "a cheerful mood for shopping".[6] Also attached to the circular were drawings that underscored the concept of product quality and gave additional tips on how to arrange the individual elements in the shop window.

By 1931, we first see evidence of retail designers such as Berger, Klinger, and Dupraz, being mentioned by name (their first names, though, are not given), in their role as guarantors of new ideas, and suggestions for window dressing and retail design. The impact of the shop window on sales was accordingly emphasized early on.[7] In the case of a certain R. Dupraz, the author is also keen to stress that the former worked in the Schönenwerd Advertising Office, in the implementation department. As a result, it is reasonable to see his recommendations as a set of concrete guidelines communicated by the *Bally* management to the respective stores, particularly by Agor Marketing A.-G., which, after its establishment in 1932, became the central organ responsible for the conception and design of advertising for *Bally* products. It is furthermore striking to note that the retail designers regularly went on research trips to cities like Paris,

New York, and London, paying particular attention to how shop-window styles in those cities captured the respective zeitgeist and flair of each place. Their impressions subsequently flowed into concrete design strategies that were published in the *Arola Hauszeitung*.

Well into the first decades of the 20th century, many shopkeepers still persevered with the traditional strategy of the so-called "stock display"—putting the widest possible range of products on show and making use of every available inch of the display area. Even though window dressing was by this time emerging as a design profession, with more sophisticated window displays being created as a result, the amassing of consumer goods behind the glass front persisted.[8] At *Bally*, too, one finds evidence of shop windows following either of these approaches, the traditional and the new, into the 1930s. Indeed, examples of both styles received awards in the *Arola Hauszeitung* for being impressive window displays. New styles of exhibition can be simultaneously observed, in the sense of the quantitative (stock) display as well as the qualitative, narrative style of window dressing [FIGS. I, II].

This means that shop windows packed with as many shoes as possible, in essence presenting the store inventory, were initially valued just as much as shop windows designed to present a specific, temporary theme. This becomes clear in a 1932 article published in the *Arola Hauszeitung*, entitled: "Schaufenster—Musterbeispiele" (Shop-Windows—Textbook Examples). Both windows of Schuhhaus Modern in Zürich are cited as valid examples. In the "Price Series Window" [FIG. I], the author highlights how effectively and clearly the 144 shoe types are put on view.[9] By contrast, the sports window, "The Mountaineering Group" [FIG. II], places the mountaineering boots in a narrative context. Here, the display makes clear visual reference to a specific event through materials and ideas that were apparently the brainchild of a certain Mr Günther, the manager of the store. The article stresses and describes in detail the manager's personal initiative of featuring the mountaineer—cut out of an existing *Bally* poster and glued to cardboard backing—alongside real granite blocks piled on top of each other and decorated with freshly plucked alpine roses and edelweiss. In conclusion, the article declares: "All these shop windows did in fact nicely bump up sales!"[10]

Two years later, the staff writer J. Honegger wrote in the *Arola Hauszeitung* encouraging managers and sales staff to visualize specific events in the window display in order to catch the eye of passers-by and bring them to a stop. Honegger advises that the appropriate themes for the window decoration should therefore be, for example, seasonal changes to the weather, and annual or temporary events. The author makes the case that variety would appeal to the regular passer-by. Honegger goes into great detail describing the window design of a francophone Swiss store manager as a shining example of a salesperson being inventive and taking the initiative.[11] The manager in question, of a store in La Chaux-de-Fonds, took the Salon d'horlogerie and Le Comptoir Industriel, two trade events which were taking place at the time, as an opportunity to present *Bally* "in the right light":

The back wall of the display window is formed by a cut-out map of the world, and wires hanging from telegraph pillars on either side of the display connect the various cities of New York, Buenos Aires, Cape Town, London, Paris, Berlin, and Vienna, with each site relating to the Bally

[III] Sample window display for the Christmas holidays (Arola Hauszeitung, no. 3, 1931, p. 9)

company and each name of the city spelled out in cut-out letters. The whole ensemble makes an impression and arouses interest among passers-by.[12]

The 1930s saw a new focus at *Bally* for window displays that incorporated an element of story-telling which was seen as an added value. Including visual references to external factors—seasons, holidays, and other events—was praised in detailed descriptions, replete with photographic documentation, as examples to be replicated by store managers and sales staff. The display space was now given over not just to the shoes available for purchase instore, but also to outside objects not even for sale that only acquired a symbolic meaning through the narrative told by the assemblage. This—at the time experimental—form of marketing was very modern and progressive [FIG. III].

The *Arola Hauszeitung* was also quick to show far more daringly abstract examples of window dressing, such as the photograph of an experimental shop window for the Christmas season designed by R. Dupraz [FIG. III].[13] This case in point is a simple arrangement of goods in a minimalistically decorated shop window featuring a trimmed selection of winter shoes and display shelves, reminiscent, at least in their pyramidal outline, of Christmas trees, with steel frames branching out on three tiers, the shoes on them almost appearing to be free-floating. The pairs placed directly on the floor are arranged beneath each metal "Tannenbaum" like presents beneath the Christmas tree. The novelty here lay in the fact that the design was neither purely narrative in content nor of the "stock display" kind. It is, however, impossible to determine whether and to what extent this window arrangement was actually adopted by *Bally* stores out in the field. The text accompanying the image suggests that sales staff should take inspiration for the coming festive season from these examples and "above all remember the decisive impact that the shop window has again and again on sales today".[14] The importance of the shop window for sales was evident in the increasingly strategically motivated discussion and distribution of advertising materials, guidelines, and out-and-out rules for window dressing with an avowedly modern look—and how this was to be implemented in creative terms.

Three main strands emerged as strategies for window dressing: quantitative merchandising (presenting as much of the product range available instore), narrative, and abstraction. What some articles preferred to outline in rather essayistic pieces of corporate journalism accompanied by photographs of shop windows, others expressed as clear instructions requiring action. The focus also now shifted away from different store managers bringing their own personal touch to window dressing towards professional retail decorators and comparisons with stores in territories much further afield, such as in Manhattan. As late as 1932, R. Dupraz wrote an article in the *Arola Hauszeitung* under the heading "Ideas That Any Salesman Worth Their Salt Would Benefit from by Putting into Practice".[15] His article outlines nine points, or rather, rules that a salesperson should follow when designing their shop window. In addition to cleanliness, order, and lighting, a frequently rotating display and a personal touch are listed as important points to remember. One idea is notably given a whole passage of its own: Not only could the store manager decorate the shop window himself, but he could do so entirely at whim and without following any advice. Most important of all, however, was point seven—this time not a suggestion, but an unavoidable, indisputable, golden rule: "Your display *must sell,* that is its sole purpose in life, and all other considerations must take a back seat to this end."[16]

Two years later, the window's commercial use was again emphasized, but this time the possibility of decorative ideas by store managers or sales staff was definitely off the table. In the article "Qu'est ce qu'une vitrine commerciale...?", published in 1934,[17] the importance of the shop window as an advertising space was pointedly described in light of increasingly aggressive competition. Window dressing became more professional, and *Bally* founded the "Department of Merchandising", which provided stores in the field with specialist staff who would know how to present the goods in the display case in a more original fashion than the competition. These retail decorators had one goal in mind: grabbing the attention of passers-by and enticing them to come inside to consider a purchase. According to the article, the decorators were expected to apply the following criteria in examining the various shoe models:

No. 1

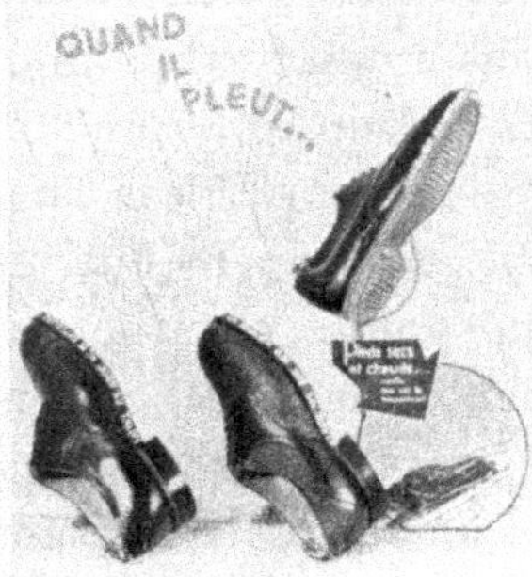

No. 2

No. 3

No. 4

Ces chiffres prouvent que la deuxième idée, très commerciale, a obtenu le meilleur résultat; aussi, le Gérant était-il tout heureux *d'avoir autorisé* son décorateur, lorsque *celui-ci lui a proposé* ces inscriptions faites à même la semelle. Un autre, par crainte de défraîchir sa marchandise aurait manqué «une bonne journée» et contrarié son «collaborateur en vitrine». Avis aux amateurs ... il faut si peu pour faire *vivre* et *parler* les beaux modèles de la grande collection «BALLY».

«Du ... re»

21

 [IV] From Arola Hauszeitung, no. 14, 1934, p. 20

1. What is special about this particular shoe?
2. What is its distinctive feature?
3. Wherein lies its value?[18]

For the article's author (and presumably its readers), it went without saying that the trained window dresser would present the product in the best possible light. The author goes on to strongly recommend that the (female) retail decorators be given the greatest possible freedom in designing the shop window to present the product in the best possible way. The author advises that even seemingly "outlandish" ideas should be accepted as long as they sell [FIG. IV].

In specific terms, the article discussed the shop-window models seen in FIG. IV and the idea of adding to each welt the inscription: "Quand il pleut ... – Et ... forcément c'est du *Bally*!" (If it rains ... it has to be *Bally*!)[19] Of these four shop windows, no. 2 reportedly achieved the best results in getting people's attention.

The new strategy of professionalized as opposed to amateur window dressing was made clear to the public at a store opening in St Gallen in 1937, expressed not merely through the storefront itself, but also in the opening speech delivered by a Mr Kuhn, during which he announced:

The jewels of any street are its shops.
The jewels of a shop are the shop windows.
The jewels in the shop windows are the goods for sale.[20]

Kuhn spoke of upheavals in architecture that were contributing to a change in the storefronts of modern businesses. Ornamentation and architectural flourishes were giving way to smooth, clear lines and surfaces, whose value was now recognizable through the use of fine materials rather than fine forms. The jewel in the façade was now the shop window, a frontage of glass for changeable displays. Thanks to *Bally's* progressive management, a number of stores and their buildings' façades had already been given a facelift, adapting them to modern tastes.[21]

This new view was undergirded by comparing the domestic situation with that of abroad. International trips were vital in this, even, for example, to as far away as the USA. Records show that such trips were not merely attended by management, but also by members of *Bally's* team of inhouse retail designers. The first trip with at least some time designated for a professional examination of the art of window dressing stateside was reported on in an issue of the *Arola Hauszeitung* in 1939. The article notes:

The decoration of the windows is very different from ours. In shops that are *au courant*, the window is given a new background four times a year. That means a new coloured background every season. [...] The storefront of department stores usually conveys a general theme. Each window then has to present a variation on this theme, each time through a different article. As a result, often only two or three pairs of shoes are displayed in any given window. The display scheme most similar to the ones back home are found in the speciality shops that are relatively few and far between, selling high-end products.[22]

In this article, published in 1939, one detects an underlying sense of uncertainty about the strategies for window dressing as practiced in the USA. However, in another article in the same staff magazine in 1948, almost a decade later, such uncertainties have all but vanished. In place of doubt, the techniques and advertising strategies of American window dressing are now roundly lauded. The European author is now keen to stress how the United States is the beacon for retailers in other territories, and "due to relentless competition is constantly forced to break new ground, which in some areas provides the lead for us to follow".[23] The megacities of the United States were centres of frenetic activity, so it naturally took a great deal more to get the inhabitants, beleaguered by the hustle and bustle of their urban environment, to show an interest in anything at all. It was therefore imperative that the basic rules of advertising be followed:

The American is positively ruthless in ensuring that this distinctive feature determined by the management (in our case the Bally-Arola unique feature of great service) is never diluted, not by anything, not even by a strong individual sense of self among staff. Because any deviation, however good it may seem in and of itself, spoils the character of the business, which is a guarantee, a mark of trust for the customers.[24]

This shows very plainly that *Bally* was more than aware of its corporate identity and the importance of upholding it, even before such a term was common currency. Furthermore, the article goes on to report that the customer base essentially fell into two categories. Most of the consumers fell into the first category, and in their case it still made sense to apply the old-school "stock display" style of window dressing in the belief that: "With enough crammed in, there's to be something for everyone."[25] This category of customer gravitated solely to the storefronts, and it was there, in public, that they searched for the right shoe. Only having found it in the window would they go in and enquire if it was in stock. And then there was the second category, the luxury, more private, clientele, who, the article explains, "go for individual elegance, who want shoes that document personality and social standing through quality, form, colour, and grace".[26]

This comparison, which can be read as a reflection of the spirit of the times, clearly shows that the window display at *Bally* was also perfectly in keeping with international standards. The simultaneity of the three different strategies—quantitative merchandising (stock display), narrative, and abstraction—was, in fact, in step with the times and consciously adapted to fit the respective clientele, whether in city or country, targeted luxury segment or general foot traffic off the main street.

1 Simmel 1990, p. 257.

2 Ibid., p. 257.

3 König 2009, p. 125.

4 Nina Schleif has provided a comprehensive study of shop-window design with her 2004 book "SchaufensterKunst", in which she examines the artistic forms, guidelines, and visual and commercial strategies adopted by window dressers in Germany and the United States from 1900 to 1960.

5 An internal staff magazine issued quarterly by Bally Arola Schuh AG. It informed its readership of company news, but also included features on fashion, travel, and recipes.

6 Circular with tips and sales advice issued by Bally-Schuhverkauf A.-G., 15 April 1948.

7 Arola Hauszeitung, no. 3, 1931, pp. 34f.

8 See Schleif 2004, p. 34.

9 Arola Hauszeitung, no. 6, 1932, p. 37.

10 Ibid., p. 37.

11 Ibid., no. 13, 1934, p. 8.

12 Ibid., p. 8.

13 Ibid., no. 3, 1931, p. 34.

14 Ibid., p. 35.

15 Ibid., no. 4, 1932, p. 18.

16 Ibid., p. 20.

17 Ibid., no. 14, 1934, pp. 20f.

18 Ibid., p. 20.

19 Ibid., pp. 20f.

20 Ibid., no. 20, 1937, p. 40.

21 Ibid., p. 40.

22 Ibid., no. 24, 1939, pp. 20f.

23 Ibid., no. 49, 1948, pp. 26f.

24 Ibid., p. 29.

25 Ibid., p. 30.

26 Ibid., p. 31.

"A Fairy-Tale Affair...!"[1]

Bally Shoes at the Swiss National Exposition of 1939[2]

Katharina Tietze

The Fashion Pavilion at the 1939 Swiss National Exposition (styled "LA39" and known colloquially as the "Landi") stood in the tradition of world expositions that included fashion design[3] long before it would ever be exhibited in museums. Having been swift to grasp the historic importance of shoes and the potential of featuring them in exhibitions, *Bally* participated at the very first Swiss national expositions, or "expos", in Zürich (1883), Geneva (1896), and Bern (1914). *Bally* also had a presence at a number of world expositions.[4] However, it is *Bally's* presentation at the LA39 that particularly stands out for its show-stopping quality.

In this essay, I will look back to this presentation of *Bally* shoes in order to reflect on the economic, political, and aesthetic aspects of trade shows.

Branded "Clothes Make People",[5] the Fashion Pavilion was situated in the modern section of the exposition on the left-hand side of the lake. The visitors entered through a fourteen-metre-tall façade, adorned with a *sgraffito* mural by Maurice Barraud showing an allegory of textile art. Visitors stepped into a world of dramatic artifice, a *mise-en-scène* with a surprise waiting to delight them around every corner. The route through the exposition kicked off in the 1000-square-metre machine hall with a very nuts-and-bolts look at fashion, including live demonstrations of the manufacture of certain fabrics. Visitors then walked through a series of about 30 rooms devoted to a variety of themes, including displays that showcased materials such as linen, straw, and artificial silk.

The exhibition was remarkable for its varied design, which was interspersed with a number of spectacular moving elements, and provided visitors with regular opportunities to digest what they'd just seen, with verdant plant-filled courtyards breaking up the route. Having first taken in the display of fabrics, both traditional and innovative, in the Textile Hall, visitors proceeded to the manufacturing section. The route concluded with displays of different accessories—including *Bally* shoes.

The building complex was designed by Karl Egender in collaboration with Bruno Giacometti. In addition to the main building—a block-like structure—the complex also comprised three round buildings with sugarloaf-shaped roofs, and the "Fashion Theatre". The latter played host in the afternoons and evenings to fashion shows and fashion-themed vaudeville performances. Even before the official opening of the LA39, the press eagerly reported on the twelve fashion models who had been specially selected and trained for the event. As the accompanying text for a publicity photograph entitled the "Day of the Lady" [FIG. 1] proclaimed: "Today, everything the modern woman requires to be 'suitably dressed' from the moment she rises to the time she goes to bed is produced by the Swiss fashion industry." Each item of footwear featured in this picture is a

[1] "Day of the Lady"; photo: F.A. Roedelberger (from Landesausstellung im Werden, Zürich 1939, p. 621)

Bally product, as were the shoes worn by the performers at the Fashion Theatre.

The *Bally* Room

Making displays of shoes look interesting comes with certain challenges. Shoes often have an appealing quality as prized and intricately crafted objects. While dresses require a form on which to be displayed, this is not the case with shoes. For the body's form is already present (in the sense of a negative) filling the space inside the shoe, which thus derives a sculptural quality. However, shoes are ordinarily in contact with the ground and are usually seen at "foot level". Displaying shoes at eye level removes them from their day-to-day context—unless they happen to be stored in a shoe closet. And since they all have broadly similar dimensions, shoes can take on a somewhat homogeneous form when displayed *en masse*. Furthermore, shoes in exhibitions are often displayed without an accompanying ensemble of clothing, which deprives them of meaningful context. Conversely, when displayed as accessories for an outfit, it is easy to overlook the shoes entirely.

For the exhibition of *Bally* footwear at the LA39, it was decided to address these issues by presenting the objects less as ordinary shoes and more like items of jewellery. The effect was achieved in a variety of ways. A room with a mirrored ceiling and one mirrored rear wall formed the backdrop for showcases whose contents were indirectly illuminated and framed with decorative cords [FIGS. II, III, IV]. Reminiscent of a Baroque picture gallery, the room appeared to stretch to infinity through the reflections of the mirrored ceiling and panelling. Even the mirror mounts, decorated with a stilettoed pump that merged with a letter "B", kept to the wider decorative theme. The shoes were positioned on transparent trays that were fitted into slots in the wall. While there was more of an emphasis on women's footwear, the display also included shoes for men and children (as well as sports shoes). A particularly eye-catching element was formed by the golden and silver-coloured evening shoes, whose dramatic effect was further enhanced by the play of mirrors. A description of the display appeared in the expo's catalogue, entitled (appropriately enough) *The Golden Book of the Landi:*

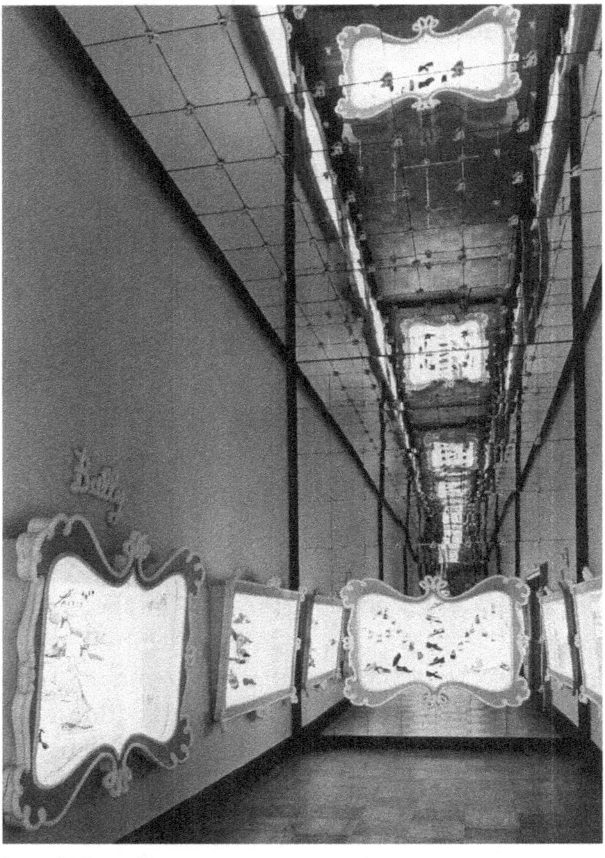

[II, III] The Bally Room
(Historical Archives of Bally Schuhfabriken AG; © Bally)

"The shoe cabinet—what a fairy-tale affair! A treasure trove in the very truest sense. [...] The gold and silver evening shoes glisten like jewels."[6]

The design legacy of Karl Egender is today held at the gta Archives at the ETH Zürich. The archive includes several pictures that illustrate the evolution of Egender's design for the *Bally* Room. One gouache shows a room with rounded corners, where variously shaped display cases are interlinked by *Bally* logos in large silver lettering [FIG. V].

Two variations of this design are detailed in Egender's perspective drawings. The first sets out a curved design [FIG. VI], while the other shows the design that was ultimately selected for a right-angled room [FIG. VII]. The spectacular visual effect created by the mirrored walls was without doubt a key factor in this selection.

Even at this preliminary stage, both versions show the display cases framed with decorative cords. Iterations of the cord's arrangement appeared at various points throughout the pavilion, where they were used in the signs for the "Fashion Theatre"

[IV] The Bally Room
(Historical Archives of Bally Schuhfabriken AG; © Bally)

and to frame the window displays in the round outbuildings located in the Fashion Pavilion's courtyard.

The archived documents also include a diagrammatic drawing detailing the arrangement of the shoes [FIG. VIII] and the final plan, dated 31 January 1939, for the design's implementation [FIG. IX]. These designs continue to include the *Bally* logo on the floor, although this detail was omitted when the pavilion was eventually built. The floorplan and profile both underline the scrupulous attention to detail in fitting the display cases to the walls. The edges of the rear panels were rounded off so that they could not be seen from the inside of the display cases, with the result that the shoes appeared to "float" on their transparent supports.

Bally shoes were thus presented in a purpose-built space that combined loving attention to detail with some eye-catchingly original design concepts.

Other Swiss shoe companies were also represented at the expo, including in one of the round pavilions. Unlike *Bally*, these presentations emulated classic commercial window displays. There is no photographic record of these rooms, which would suggest that *Bally's* display created the biggest visual impact and grabbed the most attention.

It was also possible to see *Bally* shoes beyond the confines of the Fashion Theatre and mirrored hall. As *Mitteilungen*, *Bally's* in-house company magazine, proudly reported:

[V] Karl Egender
(© gta Archives / ETH Zürich, Karl Egender)

We were delighted to see our products displayed on the Höhenstrasse [main exhibitors' avenue]: The Work and Business section featured shoes from our museum; one of our beautifully quilted boots was shown in the section on the Swiss Woman; the section on Promoting Commerce included two models [of Bally shoes] in a display showcasing Swiss exports, while two others were used as examples of "beautiful form" in the Hall of Fame. We showed Bally shoes in a display case located in the foyer of the Fashion Theatre, presenting two especially outstanding examples from our museum and current collection. And

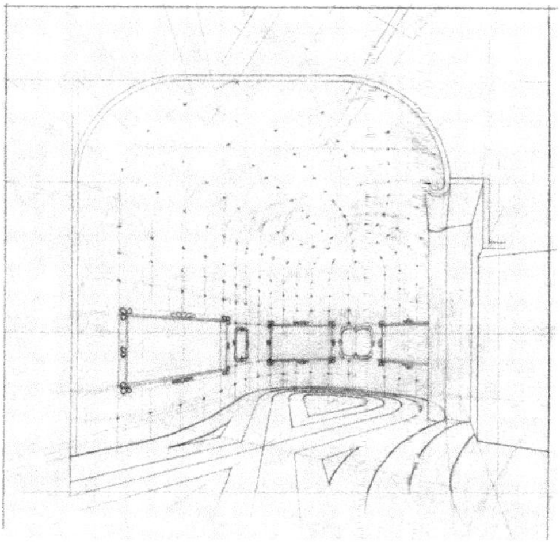

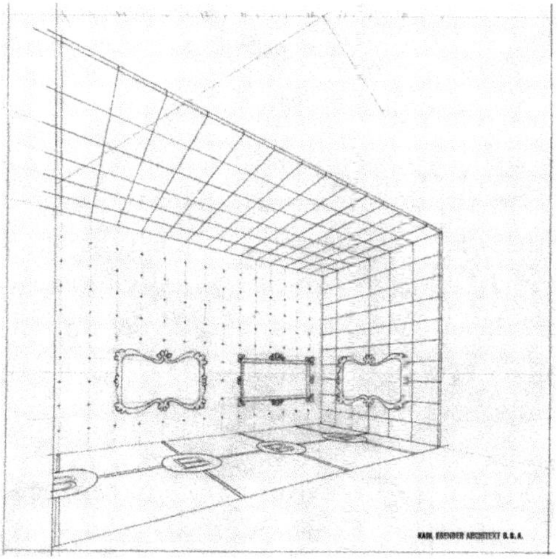

[VI, VII] Karl Egender
(© gta Archives / ETH Zürich, Karl Egender)

let us not forget the Bally shoes shown at previous events, from the Swiss National Expos of 1883, 1896, and 1914 through to the World Expo in Paris in 1937. [...] The company was even represented in the Expo Village, where a number of carp from the Bally Park [in Schönenwerd] could be seen swimming in one of the fish ponds—probably for the first time in front of such large audiences.[7]

Exports and Their Significance

The models of *Bally* shoes shown in the Export Pavilion were without doubt a far cry from the footwear sported by Swiss women in this period. The more international emphasis was already clear from the names accompanying the shoes in the display case: "Florida", "Paris", "London", "New York", and "Bally College U.S.A.". Having been given the day off to visit the LA39 expo, *Bally* employees were provided with reading material for the outing's journey to the venue. The text offered some important insights: "Our current daily output of around 11,000 pairs of shoes is only possible if a considerable portion is distributed abroad. Hence exports are of vital importance to us."[8] The article continues: "We are well aware that it's no easy task working in simple rural settings making shoes destined for spoiled and demanding city dwellers. If this visit to the National Expo helps raise awareness and improve understanding [of the role of exports], then it will have served its purpose." As the article goes on to explain:

> Just as our company is dependent on exports, so too is our entire country: it is by manufacturing products to higher standards than is possible in other countries that we earn the money needed to feed our population. If we Swiss have nothing left to offer people abroad that they cannot already procure elsewhere, then our exports will dry up and—once the nation's savings are depleted—so too any means of importing the food and raw materials needed to sustain the Swiss population. Unemployment and hunger would be the direct consequences.[9]

Here we see a resounding argument in favour of exporting fashion products, a cause passionately championed on numerous occasions during this period by Ivan Bally (1876–1965), a grandchild of the company's founder. The shoe industry had suffered in the early 1930s in the wake of the Great Depression, later exacerbated when access to export markets was curtailed by the protectionist policies of countries like France, the United Kingdom, and the United States. Then came the Second World War (the expo was still ongoing when Germany invaded Poland in September 1939). Although the war initially brought a spike in demand for utility shoes, it ultimately led to the blocking of the very trade routes on which Swiss exports depended, as Switzerland's neighbours were drawn, one by one, into the conflict. Not only were commercial considerations directly politicized, they were also (owing to *Bally* products' enhanced visibility at the expo) lent a new aesthetic dimension. Alongside his role as

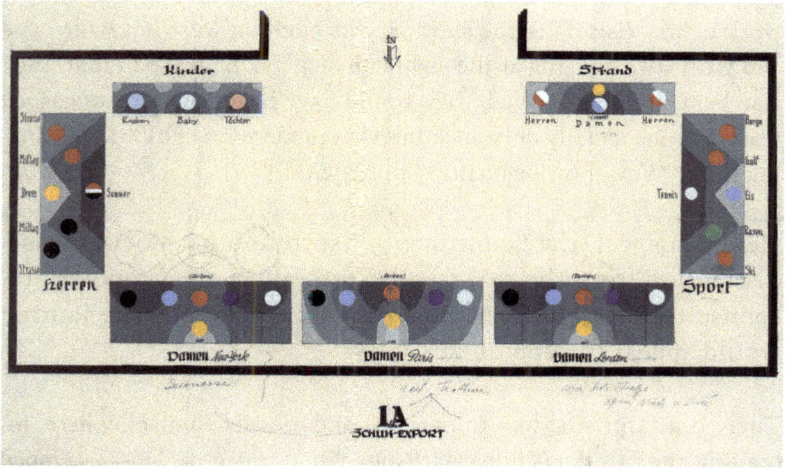

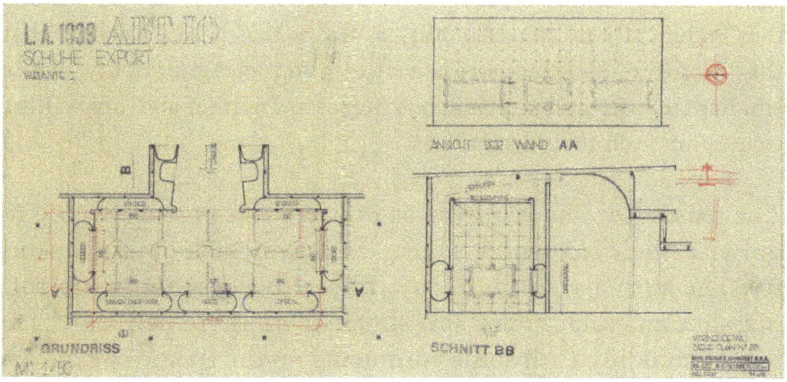

[VIII, IX] Karl Egender
(© gta Archives / ETH Zürich, Karl Egender)

company spokesman, Ivan Bally also acted as chairman of *Bally Schuhfabriken AG's* executive board from 1921 to 1954. Among his considerable additional responsibilities, Ivan Bally represented his canton by serving as a member of the Swiss Council of States from 1937 to 1943. He also authored the article on shoes that appeared in the most important publication to accompany the LA39: *Switzerland through the Mirror of the National Exposition.* Having opened with some insights about utility footwear, Ivan Bally then offered the following reflection:

As a fashion item, the shoe aspires to go one level higher. For its ambition is to be (in a thousand variations of form and colour) a miniature work of art. Visitors to the shoe exports pavilion were left wide-eyed and with jaws hanging at the sights on display. If, on top of that, they also kept their ears peeled, they would have heard the kind of gasped reactions one usually only encounters at modern art exhibitions, ranging from "Wow, how beautiful!" to "Yuck!"[10]

Here, I suspect, the "controversy" surrounding shoe art was a distraction from the real issue. Certainly, a contemporary response that appeared in the Swiss shoemakers' trade journal would appear to support this view:

There is a surprising wealth of forms and models on display here, including the latest fashions with outright bizarre designs—strapped shoes on raised cork supports (described as "buskins"), heels in forms that technically no longer qualify as heels. It is hardly credible that the "destitute" shoe industry can still afford such "gimmickry" while smaller factories and artisanal businesses are neither able nor willing to keep up with their designs.[11]

The reason the shoes proved so divisive was probably more to do with their luxurious quality at a time of looming austerity. The author goes on to pay tribute to the other participating shoe manufacturers and shoemakers more generally, before concluding with some comments on the theme of exports: "In 1938, the average value of imported shoes was 6.80 Swiss francs per pair, compared to nearly double that—12 francs—

for those exported. These figures alone give an idea of the emphasis we put on quality in this country." The writer describes the shoe as a "worthy ambassador of Swiss craftsmanship", and the LA39 as "the most effective trailblazer for our country's exports".[12]

The Landi offered Switzerland a way to forge its own national self-image. By participating at LA39, the *Bally* company was clearly asserting its identification with Swiss export culture and the international values it represented.

Fashion and Movement

Despite his analogy to modern art, Ivan Bally was most convinced by the economic benefits of featuring at the expo. However, the company also broke new ground in the presentational forms it employed at LA39. This could be seen, for example, in the approach taken to the theme of movement. A problem common to all fashion exhibitions is that clothes are displayed in a frozen state, even though, in reality, the human body is constantly moving. There were moving elements throughout the pavilion: the Textile Hall's display of Swiss fabrics (silks and St Gallen lace in particular) featured moving mannequins. Gliding as though by some magical force along a fixed path, the mannequins offered visitors a 360-degree view of their elegant dresses. One mannequin even lifted the hem of its skirt in order to give a glimpse of the petticoat beneath. As one contemporary commentator wrote: "There is not a single straight line to be seen in the interior design of this room, which is all about gentle movement."[13] The installation was designed by Robert Piguet, a Swiss *haute couture* designer who had headed his own fashion house in Paris since 1933.[14] Clothes in the Manufacturing Hall were mounted on folding panels and revealed at regular intervals in an alternating sequence of womenswear and menswear. Hats in the millinery section emerged on stands from openings in the wall. Visitors comfortably ensconced in armchairs could admire a series of hats passing before their eyes as though on a conveyor belt before vanishing back into the wall. And, as previously mentioned, visitors could see textile machines operating in the first room of the exhibition. The show was also brought to life with demonstrations of traditional handicrafts such as knitting. Headlined "The Technology of Presentation", a contemporary review in *Das Werk* magazine noted that movement "lent a more vivid quality to many of the exhibits".[15] The displays stood out for their sheer inventive variety.

Performance

By adopting a number of diverse and original approaches, the performances staged at the Fashion Theatre [FIG. X] managed to integrate movement while also responding to the challenges of exhibiting shoes as described previously. The very notion of a "Fashion Theatre" was itself unique. The theatre section of the building—indeed, the entire Fashion Pavilion—was financed by the Swiss textile industry and based on an idea originally outlined by Edgar Grieder (1891–1942), owner of the Zürich clothing store that bears his name. Addressing the organizing committee of the Swiss National Exposition in 1938, he wrote:

[x] Fashion Theatre
(Historical Archives of Bally Schuhfabriken AG; © Bally)

> The guiding principle should be to create displays that bring the fashion industry to life. Relying on a rigid format to present "fashion" as the epitome of transformation is an absurdity in and of itself; nor would there be any sense in requiring fashion houses such as ours, which already owns a store front on Bahnhofstrasse, to hire additional display windows at an exhibition—only then to use the space for displaying the same fashions over a period of several months (changing the display on a weekly basis, as demanded by the fashion columns to which our industry is beholden, is not possible due to technical reasons). The only suitable and entertaining way to present anything "fashion"-related is therefore to stage a daily changing programme of fashion shows featuring real-life models.[16]

In addition to putting these ideas into practice, Grieder also determined the organizational and financial form ultimately assumed by the project when he proposed the creation of a co-operative.

The theatre seated 280 people and was equipped with a revolving stage configured so that no one in the audience would find themselves sitting more than ten metres from the performers. The stage was draped in grey artificial silk and illuminated by 1500 small lights. The roof was retractable, and "in the adjoining bar, there was an attempt to bring together elements of Baroque plaster moulding with Surrealist painting".[17]

All the performers wore *Bally* footwear, which meant the shoes could be seen fulfilling their intended function: as accessories complementing particular "looks". When used as props—in a suitcase full of shoes, for example—they played a more active role, almost becoming characters in the performance. Shoes also occupied a key role in the narrative. In contrast to the exhibition of luxury shoes, the performances addressed a wide range of socio-economic backgrounds. In one song, a shoe-shiner describes his all-consuming work: He dreams about having to polish a thousand pairs of shoes and is resigned to there being no respite to his work even in heaven. The refrain lists various types of shoes—small and large, old and new, shoes with well-worn heels, and shoes for dancing. The rather melancholy ditty concludes in loose translation: "And I clean 'em all, all, all / But it's *Bally* I like best of all."

The second performance included another shoe-related musical number, this time about the importance of suitable footwear. Two elegantly attired couples are all set to head for the mountains, but are lucky enough to be stopped before venturing onto a glacier without the necessary mountain shoes [FIG. XI]. The story finished with a song whose title translates as "Heel in the Snow", sung by Zarli Carigiet [FIG. XII], which is about pairs of shoes and how they make the perfect match. The song concludes with lines that read something like this: "Take that good old climbing boot, for example. All it needs is the same as the [lady's] shoe: the *Bally* stamp!"

Shoes were also the visual centrepiece of the third vaudeville act, where they appeared in a format that called to mind a TV screen (a cutting-edge medium in this period). Legs appeared together in a frame, each pair showcasing a different pair of shoes. "An ingenious display of shoe fashions, which often left visitors unable to decide what they found more attractive—the shoes, or the beautiful legs [...]"[18] [FIG. XIII]. Accompanying the "television" performance was music originally composed by Paul Burkhard.[19] A woman places an order over the telephone, having had her interest piqued by an advertisement promoting shoes with names like "Blue Nile" and "Firebird". She comments guiltily: "This will be the death of me!"—to which the saleswoman on the line quips: "Shoes couldn't possibly be the death of any-

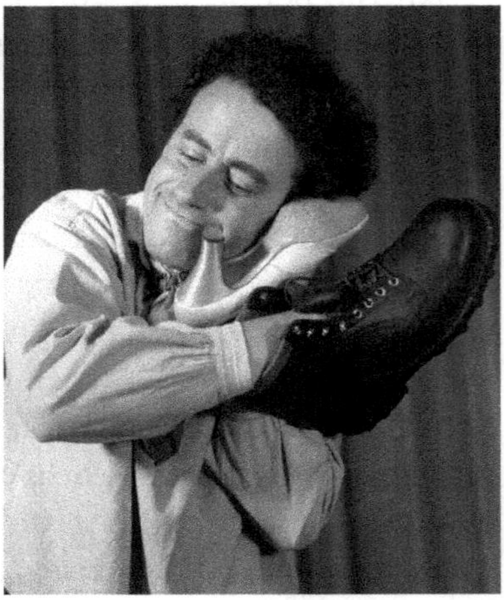

[XI, XII] Scenes from the Fashion Theatre with Zarli Carigiet (Historical Archives of Bally Schuhfabriken AG; © Bally)

one." The woman then telephones her lover, whom she calls by turns "George", "Alexander", and finally even "Othello". He in turn serenades his beloved with a song, which concludes: "You're my happiness, my salvation. But look a little closer and you'll see, what I love is not so much you—but your shoe." The young woman is not only characterized by her love of shoes and flirtatious nature, but also by her familiarity with the latest technology—the telephone.

As one account put it: "It was no small task to solve the problem we had set ourselves: namely, putting on a *theatrical advertisement* that was easy on both the eyes and ears. [...] This was advertising dressed up to the nines in its most elegant dress: dazzling in its variety, sparking with effervescent humour."[20] Swiss fashion manufacturers provided the raw material for individual scenes, with the products explored as dramatic themes. The performances functioned as a kind of performative display window—a live advertisement, as it were. Advertisement or not, *Bally* made sure to cast stars from Switzerland's cabaret and entertainment industry who were big names, delivering polished acts. The result was a unique genre that synthesized art and commerce. As for the building itself, the Fashion Theatre was an entirely unique concept; then as now, fashion shows were held in rooms normally used for other purposes.

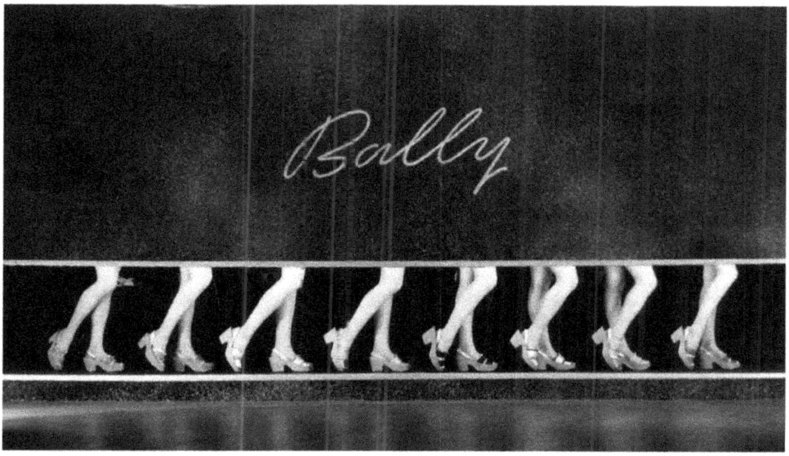

[XIII] Fashion Theatre
(Historical Archives of Bally Schuhfabriken AG; © Bally)

Fashion and Architecture

Five years previously, the Fashion Pavilion's architect, Karl Egender, had designed the Kunstgewerbeschule in Zürich (today part of the ZHdK, Zürich University of the Arts)—a wonderfully functional building designed in the International Style. From an aesthetic point of view, the "Clothes Make People" pavilion diverged in a number of ways from this earlier building. Yet there were also similarities: For example, both buildings boasted bright passageways connecting the interior to outdoor spaces (which were in turn filled with plants and sculptures). Attached to the building on the LA39 site and set within a garden, the three round structures could be described as the pavilion's "landmark" feature, visible from afar. They were built of wood, like the majority of buildings at the LA39. Topped with cone-shaped roofs dotted with small cutouts in the form of rhombuses, their form was strikingly enigmatic. The shape, not unlike a tajine, lent the buildings an air of exoticism. Erected in the gardens in front of the expo pavilion, the buildings had a sculptural appearance reminiscent of billowing skirts. The rhombus pattern might be interpreted as a reference to lace (which was, after all, one of Switzerland's major textile products) [FIG. XIV].

Contemporary Reactions

Prior to attempting to interpret the architecture, it is first useful to have some idea of the character of "Landi style" (as the prevailing aesthetic at the exposition was termed). A comprehensive overview of this style was presented in a review of the Swiss National Exposition published by *Das Werk* magazine. The review's author was Peter Meyer, who, in addition to editing the magazine from 1930 to 1942, was himself an extremely eloquent architectural critic. A significant motivation for Swiss architects in this period was the urge to take a symbolic stand against the monumentalist architecture of the country's fascist neighbours. One aspect of this was the idea of favouring open spaces over enclosed cubes, as exemplified in the combination of internal courtyards and building annexes seen at the Fashion Pavilion. Furthermore, the Fashion Theatre boasted a retractable roof and hence an "open space" in its most literal sense.

The pavilion's design adopted other trademark "Landi style" features. For example, true to the guiding principle that enjoined architects to create "an entrance—not a portal", visitors entered the pavilion through a simple door rather than some grand ceremonial gate. Even then, and in keeping with the style's systematic avoidance of symmetry, the doors were not positioned centrally. The design was also characterized by its emphasis on movement, airiness, and transparency. As an example of the sort of floating ceilings that conveyed these qualities, the article refers to the Fashion Pavilion's "light-blue ceiling that undulates over the long corridor". There was also an airy quality to the "disembodied supports"[21] that functioned as an architectural alternative to Neoclassical columns. The review also praises the "varied surface structures made up of battens, grids, and geometric patterns".[22] Thus, for example, board-and-batten sidings were used for the outer walls of the conical wooden buildings. The battens under the roof were singled out for having a "directly proportional relationship to the human body, being of a width that roughly matched the size of the human hand".[23] Battening was also one way of making structural materials visible at the surface, substituting ornamentation, which was to be avoided. The only ornamentation to speak of was the

[XIV] Fashion Pavilion
(© Schweizerisches Sozialarchiv, F Fb-0021-42)

"surface patterning in the form of rhomboids painted in straight lines at perspectival angles".[24] This was another innovative design element that could be seen incorporated into the Fashion Pavilion.

Another article praises the exhibition's "thematic principle". This did not allow for decorative forms, "or rather, only as exceptions that merely emphasized the rule—on display for example at the Fashion Pavilion, where the theme of playfulness and luxury is the very point of the exhibit". On the other hand, the article notes: "The use of movement in a number of displays fosters a greater sense of immediacy." The mannequins and revolving wall panels were cited as examples of this approach.[25]

The article was more critical of the way visitors were channelled into a "compulsory route", complaining that "in the Fashion Pavilion [...] one occasionally felt as though one had fallen into a trap". The article goes on to bemoan how "anyone wishing to show Bally shoes to an acquaintance has first to walk a good few kilometres through all the fabrics displays".[26] It was perhaps inevitable that critical responses would not be universally positive in view of the experimental spirit in which the pavilion was constructed. But overall, as a theme, fashion was particularly well suited to seeing new architectural ambitions put into practice.

Artistic Contributions

Another aspect of the Swiss National Expo that attracted responses from critics was the relationship between free and applied art. "Abstract art—applied: Practically all formal elements of 'non-representational' art have been incorporated into the detail of the decor",[27] wrote Meyer, in a comment that left no doubt about his scepticism towards abstract art. However, LA39 does appear to have been more a celebration of applied art than "free" or fine art. The various sculptures (including a large number of female nudes) and murals tended towards the very monumentality that the architecture strove to avoid. A more modestly scaled contribution from a major Swiss artist was rejected. Bruno Giacometti, one of Karl Egender's assistants, had hoped to display a sculpture by his brother, Alberto, in one of the inner courtyards. Alberto Giacometti proposed using one of the pedestals to display a very small figure, arguing "it matters not whether a figure is big or small, the only important consideration is that it should dominate the space".[28] However, the proposal was rejected in favour of another of the artist's works, *Cube* (1933), which, according to his brother Bruno, was the sole example of abstract sculpture anywhere at the expo.[29] There are tellingly no photographs of this courtyard, as perhaps befits its status as an aesthetic outlier. However, there are pictures of another courtyard where a monumental head by Cornelia Forster was displayed in front of wooden slats that, by a trick of perspective, appeared to be mounted on the wall, and at whose centre was a Surrealist-inspired picture. Commissions were awarded to visual artists whose works then contributed to the overall aesthetic impact—to the point where it was not always possible to hone in and distinguish the "art" from the "design". Just as this creative divide was bridged, so too were the respective responses of specialist and lay audiences. As Peter Meyer remarked: "For the first time, the unholy chasm dividing 'experts' (that is, artists, architects, and art-savvy intellectuals) on the one hand, and the 'general public' unversed in art criticism on the other has begun to close."[30]

Conclusion

The practice of exhibiting consumer products began with the World's Fairs of the mid-19th century. The first to include contemporary fashions was probably the 1900 Exposition Universelle in Paris, where visitors could admire the latest designs at the Pavillon de la Mode. The exposition in Paris was also the setting for the Palais de la Costume, which marked the first attempt to create a global narrative of fashion and costume history. Visitors to the pavilion could see wax figures dressed in reproductions of historical clothing, displayed in settings designed to evoke the respective period.[31] These early displays only included footwear as accessories, and it was not until the 1930s that the history of shoe exhibitions began in earnest. In 1934, the Ferargil Galleries in New York held an exhibition on the theme of feet and shoes. Visitors to the venue (a private gallery, and thus in essence a salesroom of sorts) could admire drawings, paintings, and sculptures alongside shoes designed by André Perugia.[32] In 1941, the Museum of Costume Art (the future Costume Institute of New York's Metropolitan Museum) organized an exhibition of 18th-century shoes, stockings, and other accessories. To date, however, there have been no publications on the history of shoe exhibitions.

It was not until the turn of the millennium that fashion exhibitions attracted any significant academic scrutiny.[33] Bulking large in this field are the respective histories of the important fashion departments at the Victoria & Albert Museum in London and the Metropolitan Museum in New York. Two exhibitions in particular stand out as seminal moments: In 1971, Cecil Beaton curated *Fashion: An Anthology* in London,[34] then two years later came the opening of Diane Vreeland's *The World of Balenciaga* in New York.[35] As Gertrud Lehnert has underlined, commercial and non-commercial shows—expos of trade and industry and curatorial retrospectives—have continually served as mutual sources of inspiration and influence, to the extent that it is nowadays not always possible to make a clear distinction between the two.

Having hosted an exhibition entitled simply *The Shoe* back in 1915, the Kunstgewerbemuseum Zürich (now Museum für Gestaltung) was early to recognize the shoe's potential as a museum exhibit. It also held the exhibition *The Shoe: The History of Its Manufacture and Use* in 1936/37. The majority of the exhibits at both shows was either *Bally* products or shoes loaned from the company's collection of historical models.[36] The latter formed the basis for the *Bally* Shoe Museum in Schönenwerd, which opened in 1942 at the former home of the company's founder and finally gave members of the public the opportunity to see this comprehensive (and, still today, remarkable) collection. These various initiatives enjoyed a symbiotic relationship, as institutions continued to accumulate experience and draw lessons from different approaches to exhibiting.

The pavilion at LA39 exemplified an especially original approach to displaying fashion in general and shoes in particular. There are a number of reasons why the different methods of displaying exhibits were so varied and accomplished. As a company, *Bally* was already a veteran of holding exhibitions, while the involvement of a figure like Edgar Grieder lent real momentum to the project. With an architect at the helm of LA39 and the creative talents of Karl Egender put to work on the Fashion Pavilion, it was possible to break new ground in the realm of exhibition design. Furthermore, the wider geopolitical context created the need to develop a distinct and independent aesthetic idiom—for which the theme of fashion was particularly well suited (hence, for example, the display's focus on the role of movement in fashion). Finally, fashion was of significant value to the Swiss economy, with textile machines, silk, lace, and footwear numbering among the country's major exports. These various factors made for a multifaceted fashion exhibition characterized by a wide array of innovative ideas for which no expense was spared.

It was on the back of these experiences that the Swiss Fashion Week first came into being. Held annually in Zürich from 1942 to 1944, this event similarly benefited from the expertise of Karl Egender as senior architect. Once again, *Bally* shoes enjoyed a prominent place and were displayed with similar creative flair. Moreover, the company's wealth of experience in participating in trade shows and expos would certainly have been an advantage when it opened the *Bally* Shoe Museum in 1942.

In the boardroom, however, enthusiasm for the exhibition was initially rather muted, as is clear from the minutes of a meeting held on 12 October 1938: "Mr Max Bally fails to see how participating at the National Expo will help increase sales to a level that could justify the high costs (probably in the order of 60,000 Swiss francs)." However, when the board subsequently discussed the dissolution of the Fashion Theatre cooperative, members took the view that "the Fashion Theatre [had been] a success [...] and without doubt one of the crowning features of the Landi".

1 "Eine märchenhafte Angelegenheit!"; Freitag 1939, p. 157.

2 I have previously described the Fashion Pavilion in an abridged version of this text. See: "Kleider machen Leute. Der Modepavillon auf der Schweizerischen Landesausstellung" in: Jahrbuch ntm; Augsburg 2018.

3 An example of this was the 1900 Exposition Universelle in Paris, where the latest fashions could be admired at the Pavillion de la Mode. See Clark/De la Haye 2014, p. 11.

4 For example, the expositions at Chicago (1933/34), Brussels (1935), Paris (1937), and New York (1938).

5 The pavilion's name derives from the title of a novella by Gottfried Keller in which the protagonist's deceptively elegant attire results in him becoming unwittingly embroiled in a confidence trick. Although portrayed in a far from positive light, fashion nonetheless emerges in the story as a force to be reckoned with.

6 Freitag 1939, p. 157.

7 Mitteilungen der Bally-Schuhfabriken A.-G., 15 November 1939, pp. 2f.

8 Ibid., 1 June 1939, p. 2.

9 Ibid., p. 3.

10 Bally 1940, p. 143.

11 Schweizerische Schuhmacher-Zeitung, year 65, no. 12, 15 June 1939, p. 182.

12 Ibid., p. 146.

13 Wagner 1939, p. 140.

14 Christian Dior first cut his teeth as a fashion designer at Piguet's studio, where he worked from 1938 to 1939.

15 Anon. 1939, p. 347.

16 The Edgar Grieder estate, Zürich City Archives.

17 Oboussier 1940, p. 621.

18 Trapp: "Das Modetheater und sein Drum und Dran" in: Festliche Landi, p. 60.

19 Programme booklet, Historical Archives of Bally Schuhfabriken AG, Schönenwerd.

20 Zuppinger 1940, p. 575.

21 Das Werk, vol. 11, 1939, p. 332.

22 Ibid., p. 334.

23 Ibid., p. 334.

24 Ibid., p. 336.

25 Anon: Die Technik der Darstellung, 1939, p. 347.

26 Ibid., p. 348.

27 Ibid., p. 345.

28 Baumann 2009, p. 45.

29 Küster 2009, p. 93.

30 P.M.: "Die Architektur der Landesausstellung--kritische Besprechung", 1939, p. 321.

31 For more on this subject, see Clark/De la Haye 2014, pp. 11f.

32 Steele/Hill 2012, p. 39.

33 Lehnert/Kühl/Weise 2014.

34 Clark/De la Haye 2014.

35 Koda/Glasscock 2014.

36 This tradition provided the source materials for a research project, the fruits of which were shown at the exhibition "Bally—Swiss Shoes since 1851" at the Museum für Gestaltung, Zürich.

Contributors

Henriette-Friederike Herm is assistant lecturer at Zürich University of the Arts (ZHdK). She studied fashion design in Hamburg and design at Zürich University of the Arts.

Anna-Brigitte Schlittler is art historian and lecturer at Zürich University of the Arts (ZHdK) and F+F Schule für Kunst und Design. She has studied art history, history, and philosophy at the University of Zürich. Her research focuses on history and theory of fashion.

Daniel Späti studied product design at Zürich University of the Arts (ZHdK) and worked for six years in product development and design at Bally. He is a senior lecturer at ZHdK and head of Shared Campus, a transcultural and cross-disciplinary collaboration platform by seven art universities from Asia and Europe. He became a research associate in 2012. His main research field is event culture and city development.

Katharina Tietze is professor of design at Zürich University of the Arts (ZHdK) and head of the Trends & Identity programme. She studied fashion design at Berlin University of the Arts. Her research focuses on fashion, everyday culture, and identity.

Roman Wild is a historian and university lecturer. His dissertation *Auf Schritt und Tritt. Der schweizerische Schuhmarkt 1918–1948* was published in 2019. He is currently finishing a book on the history of the Zürich silk industry since 1800 at Lucerne University of Applied Sciences and Arts.

Bibliography

Archival Material

Bally Archives Schönenwerd

Agor AG Zürich, Jahresbericht & Bilanz 1935.

Agor AG Zürich, Jahresbericht & Bilanz 1939.

Agor AG, Kontrollblätter mit Inseraten für die Bally-Filialen.

Arola AG, Bericht an die Direktion über das Geschäftsjahr 1934/35.

Bally, Eduard: "Bd. 1: Geschichte C.F. Bally AG; Bd. 2: Statistische Tabellen"; Schönenwerd 1925 [on CD-ROM].

Bally Lyon, Ordner mit 33 Fotos zur Produktion von Holzsohlen-Schuhen.

Bally Sportausstellung, M.P.F., 1935.

Bally Verkaufskataloge 1880–1930.

Bally Direktionsprotokolle 1926–1947.

[Anon.]: "Gleitschutz von Caesar bis zur Himalaya-Expedition"; ca. 1950.

Programmheft LA 39.

Stöckli, Albert: Militärschuhe, ca. 1972.

Ballyana Archives Schönenwerd

Bally, Max: "Gedanken zur Entwicklung des Ballyschuhs", 24.11.1969; Streuli Bequest M./P-SM/1.

Bally, Max: "Eindrücke über die führenden USA Schuhunternehmen anlässlich meiner Herbstreise 1954", pp. 12–14; P-WB/7.

Oboussier, Marc: "Die Probleme der Kreationsabteilung"; Streuli Bequest P-SM/1.

Stadtarchiv Zürich

The Edgar Grieder Estate.

Stiftung Historisches Material der Schweizer Armee (HAM)

Laubacher/HAM 2007/13

Literature

Amsler, André: 'Wer dem Werbefilm verfällt, ist verloren für die Welt'. Das Werk von Julius Pinschewer 1883–1961; Zürich: Chronos 1997.

Andreozzi, Luciano / Bianchi, Marina: "Fashion. Why People Like It and Theorists Do Not", in: Marina Bianchi (ed.): The Evolution of Consumption. Theories and Practices; Amsterdam: Elsevier 2007, pp. 209–230.

Angst, Kenneth: Von der alten zur neuen Gewerbepolitik. Liberalkorporative Neuorientierung des Schweizerischen Gewerbeverbandes (1930–1942); Zürich and Bamberg: Difo 1992.

[Anon.]: "Das Jahr 1930", in: Schweizerische Schuhmacher-Zeitung 56 (1931), p. 17.

[Anon.]: "Ist der ständige Modewechsel nützlich oder schädlich?", in: Der Schuhhandel 19 (1936), Nr. 13, pp. 188f.

[Anon.] (P.M.): "Die Architektur der Landesausstellung – kritische Besprechung", in: Das Werk 11 (1939), pp. 321–324.

[Anon.]: "Stilkriterien der modernen Architektur an der LA", in: Das Werk 11 (1939), pp. 330–339.

[Anon.]: "Die Technik der Darstellung", in: Das Werk 11 (1939), pp. 345–349.

[Anon.] (F.S.): "Vom Schuh und seiner Entstehung"; Separatdruck aus: Neue Zürcher Zeitung, 27. August 1941.

[Anon.]: "Die volkswirtschaftlichen Schäden von Fußkrankheiten", in: Der Schuhhandel 25 (1942), p. 29.

[Anon.]: "Modeschuh in der Mangelwirtschaft", in: Der Schuhhandel 25 (1942), p. 106.

Arends, Paul C.: Das ABC der Kunstseiden und Zellwollen; Berlin: Paul C. Arends 1940.

Arni, Marco: Es drückt der Schuh – die Fussbekleidungsfrage in der Schweizer Armee 1850–1918; Bern: Schriftenreihe der Eidgenössischen Militärbibliothek und des Historischen Dienstes 2010.

Arola Hauszeitung 1931–1959.

Bally, Iwan: "Vom Schuh, einst und jetzt", in: Armin Meili (ed.): Die Schweiz im Spiegel der Landesausstellung; Zürich 1940, pp. 142–146.

Bally Arola Service (ed.): Die Arola-Schuh AG. 25 Jahre Bally Arola Service. Zur Erinnerung an das 25-jährige Bestehen unserer Firma; Zürich 1946.

Bally Schuhfabriken AG (ed.): Hundert Jahre Bally-Schuhe, 1851–1951. Allen unseren Angestellten und Arbeitern in dankbarer Anerkennung ihrer treuen Mitarbeit und Verdienste gewidmet; Schönenwerd 1951.

Barthes, Roland: "Plastic", in: Dietmar Rübel et al. (ed.): Materialästhetik. Quellentexte zu Kunst, Design und Architektur; Berlin: Reimer 2005, pp. 87–89.

Bauer, Robert: Das Jahrhundert der Chemiefasern; Munich: Goldmann 1958.

Baumann, Felix: Bruno Giacometti erinnert sich. Gespräche mit Felix Baumann; Zürich: Scheidegger & Spiess 2009.

Baumann Püntener, Karin: "Wider die Fluktuation. Die Strategien des Unternehmens Bally zur Bildung einer Stammarbeiterschaft", in: Ulrich Pfister / Brigitte Studer / Jakob Tanner (eds.): Arbeit im Wandel – travail en mutation. Deutung, Organisation und Herrschaft vom Mittelalter bis zur Gegenwart – Interprétation, organisation et pouvoir, du Moyen Age à nos jours; Schweizerisches Jahrbuch für Wirtschafts- und Sozialgeschichte / Annuaire suisse d'histoire économique et sociale, Bd. 14; Zürich: Chronos 1996, pp. 223–232.

Baumgarten-Tramer, Franziska: "Psychohygiene und Mode", in: Gesundheit und Wohlfahrt 18 (1938), pp. 627–640.

Benstock, Shari / Ferriss, Suzanne (eds.): Footnotes on Shoes; New Brunswick etc.: Rutgers University Press 2001. https://doi.org/10.2752/136270402779615343

Berry, Jess: House of Fashion. Haute Couture and the Modern Interior; London etc.: Bloomsbury 2018. https://doi.org/10.5040/9781474283427

Bill, Max (hrsg. von der Direktion der Schweizer Mustermessen): Die gute Form – 6 Jahre Auszeichnung "Die gute Form" an der Schweizer Mustermesse in Basel; Winterthur: Buchdruckerei Winterthur 1957.

Black, Sandy et al. (eds.): The Handbook of Fashion Studies; London etc.: Bloomsbury 2013.

Blaszczyk, Regina Lee: Imagining Consumers. Design and Innovation from Wedgwood to Corning; Baltimore and London: The Johns Hopkins University Press 2000. https://doi.org/10.1353/book.72312

Blaszczyk, Regina Lee: The Color Revolution; Cambridge Mass. and London: The MIT Press 2012. https://doi.org/10.7551/mitpress/8762.001.0001

Blaszczyk, Regina Lee: "The Hidden Spaces of Fashion Production", in: Sandy Black et al. (eds.): The Handbook of Fashion Studies; London etc.: Bloomsbury 2013, pp. 181–196.

Blaszczyk, Regina Lee (ed.): Producing Fashion. Commerce, Culture, and Consumers; Philadelphia: University of Pennsylvania Press 2008. https://doi.org/10.9783/9780812206050

Blaszczyk, Regina Lee / Wubs, Ben (eds.): The Fashion Forecasters. A Hidden History of Color and Trend Prediction; London etc.: Bloomsbury 2018. https://doi.org/10.5040/9781350017191

Blatter, Max: Alles über Schuhe; Schweizerischer Schuhhändler-Verband 2001.

Bochsler, Regula: "Der Migros-Gründer und seine volkswirtschaftliche Beraterin", in: Elisabeth Joris/Bruno Meier/Martin Widmer (ed.): Historische Begegnungen. Biografische Essays zur Schweizer Geschichte; Baden: hier + jetzt 2014, pp. 236–259.

Bochsler, Regula / Derungs, Pascal (eds.): Und führe uns in Versuchung. 100 Jahre Schweizer Werbefilm; Zürich: Edition Museum für Gestaltung 1998.

Breyer, Nike: "'Es gibt keinen gesunden Menschenfuß, der vorn in einer Spitze ausläuft' (Knud Ahlborn) – Wandervögel, Jugendbewegung und Schuhreform", in: Medizin, Gesellschaft und Geschichte 30, 2011, pp. 85–110.

Breyer, Nike U.: Schritt für Schritt – Die Geburt des modernen Schuhs; Ingolstadt: Deutsches Medizinhistorisches Museum 2012.

Büchi, H.: Aus der Heimat des Bally-Schuhs. Ein Gang durch die Bally-Schuhfabriken Aktiengesellschaft Schönenwerd (Schweiz); Berlin: Max Schröder 1930 [Sonderdruck aus: Internationale Industrie-Bibliothek 40, 1930].

Burlet, Jürg: "Die Militärschuhe im 20. Jahrhundert", in: Tanzbödler 25, Nr. 88, 2008, pp. 12–24.

Clark, Judith / de la Haye, Amy: Exhibiting Fashion. Before and After 1971; New Haven: Yale University Press 2014.

Cross, Nigel: Designerly Ways of Knowing; Basel etc.: Birkhäuser 2007.

Daub, Edelgard: Franziska Baumgarten. Eine Frau zwischen akademischer und praktischer Psychologie; Frankfurt on the Main: Peter Lang 1996.

David, Helene: "Bedeutung und Probleme des modernen Hausfrauenberufes", in: Zweiter Schweizerischer Kongress für Fraueninteressen (ed.): Bericht; Bern: Stämpfli 1921, pp. 92–113.

Droux, Joëlle: "Rationnement et consommation en Suisse (1939–1945)", in: Alain Chatriot / Marie-Emmanuelle Chessel / Matthew Hilton (eds.): Au nom du consommateur. Consommation et politique en Europe et aux Etats-Unis au XXe siècle; Paris: Ed. La Découverte 2004, pp. 63–79.

Duttweiler, Gottlieb: Luxussteuern; Zürich: City Druck 1942.

Ebert, Christoph: Beschreibung und Bewertung der Funktionalität von Sportprodukten; Munich 2010 (unpublished dissertation, TU Munich).

Eidgenössisches Volkswirtschaftsdepartement (ed.): Der Schuhhandel in der Schweiz; Bern 1946 [Veröffentlichung der Preisbildungskommission des Eidgenössischen Volkswirtschaftsdepartementes, 26].

Freitag, Maria: "Kleider machen Leute", in: Julius Wagner (ed.): Das goldene Buch der LA; Zürich 1939, pp. 139–163.

Gasser, Elsa F.: "Zürcher Index der Bekleidungskosten", in: Zürcher Statistische Nachrichten, 1 (1924), pp. 117–129.

Gaugele, Elke: "Modetheorien und Fashion Studies", in: Elke Gaugele / Jens Kastner (ed.): Critical Studies. Kultur- und Sozialtheorie im Kunstfeld; Wiesbaden: Springer 2016, pp. 183–207. https://doi.org/10.1007/978-3-658-10412-2_11

Gnägi, Thomas et al. (ed.): Gestaltung Werk Gesellschaft. 100 Jahre Schweizerischer Werkbund SWB; Zürich 2013.

Godau, Marion: Produktdesign. Eine Einführung mit Beispielen aus der Praxis; Basel: Birkhäuser 2004.

Godley, Andrew / Kershen, Anne / Schapiro, Raphael: "Fashion and Its Impact on the Economic Development of London's East End Womenswear Industry, 1929–62. The Case of Ellis and Goldstein", in: Textile History 2 (2003), pp. 214–228. https://doi.org/10.1179/004049603235001535

Grassmann, W. et al.: Handbuch der Gerbereichemie und Lederfabrikation. Dritter Band, 1. Teil: Zurichtung und Prüfung des Leders; Vienna: Springer 1936.

Hawes, Elizabeth: Fashion Is Spinach. How to Beat the Fashion Racket; Chicago: APA Publications 2015 [New York 1938].

Heim, Arnold: "Schuhe oder Füße? Ein Mahnruf", in: Die Alpen 17/1 (1941), pp. 1–4.

Heim, Arnold: "Nochmals: Schuhe oder Füße. Eine Antwort von Arnold Heim", in: Die Alpen 17/3 (1941), pp. 54f.

Heim, Arnold: Weltbild eines Naturforschers. Mein Bekenntnis; Bern: Huber 1942.

Heim, Arnold: "Schuhe oder Füße?", in: Tages-Anzeiger für Stadt und Kanton Zürich, 28.9.1956.

Heim, Peter: Königreich Bally. Fabrikherren und Arbeiter in Schönenwerd; Baden: hier + jetzt 2000.

Heller, Eva: Wie Farben wirken; Reinbek: Rowohlt 1989.

Hengartner, Eugen: Sportgerät Skischuh; Jahrbuch des Schweiz. Ski-Verbandes [Separatdruck für Arola-Schuh AG], n.y.

Honeyman, Katrina / Godley, Andrew: "Introduction. Doing Business with Fashion", in: Textile History 34 (2003), pp. 101–106. https://doi.org/10.1179/004049603235001562

Jaun, Rudolf: Management und Arbeiterschaft. Verwissenschaftlichung, Amerikanisierung und Rationalisierung der Arbeitsverhältnisse in der Schweiz 1873–1959; Zürich: Chronos 1986.

Kamber, Walter: "Nachklänge zum Besuche der Schuhfabrik Bally vom 17. April 1933", in: Information Arola Hauszeitung 3 (1933), pp. 22–27.

Kaufmann, Max: "Fünfundzwanzig Jahre Preisbildungskommission", in: Die Volkswirtschaft 25 (1952), pp. 248f.

Kaufmann, Peter: "Schlusswort des Präsidenten Peter Kaufmann", in: Gesellschaft für Marktforschung (ed.): Betriebsprobleme der Mode; Zürich 1944, pp. 29–33.

Keun, Irmgard: Das kunstseidene Mädchen; Berlin: Ullstein 2004 [1932].

Klaus, Fred J.: Das BALLY-Lehrstück. Ein Insider-Bericht; Zürich: Orell Füssli 1985.

Klinger, Hans: "Plauderei über einen Mode-Photowettbewerb", in: Schweizer Reklame und Schweizer graphische Mitteilungen 46 (1942), pp. 193–196.

Koda, Harold / Glasscock, Jessica: "The Costume Institute at The Metropolitan Museum of Art. An Evolving History", in: Marie Riegels Melchior / Birgitta Svensson (eds.): Fashion and Museums. Theory and Practice; London: Bloomsbury 2014, pp. 21–32. https://doi.org/10.5040/9781350050914.ch-001

König, Gudrun M.: Konsumkultur. Inszenierte Warenwelt um 1900; Vienna: Böhlau 2009.

König, Gudrun M. (ed.): Alltagsdinge. Erkundungen der materiellen Kultur; Tübingen: Tübinger Vereinigung für Volkskunde 2005.

König, Gudrun M. / Papierz, Zuzanna: "Plädoyer für eine qualitative Dinganalyse", in: Sabine Hess / Johannes Moser / Maria Schwertl (eds.): Europäisch-ethnologisches Forschen. Neue Methoden und Konzepte; Berlin: Reimer 2012, pp. 283–307.

Kotik, Jan: Konsum oder Verbrauch. Versuch über Gebrauchswert und Bedürfnisse; Hamburg: Hoffmann und Campe 1974.

Kurtzig, K.: "Die Arten des Werbefilmes", in: Industrielle Psychotechnik 10 (1926), pp. 310–314.

Küster, Ulf: "Monumentalität kontra Gigantismus", in: Du 797, Juni 2009, pp. 89–93.

Lakoff, George / Johnson, Mark: Leben in Metaphern. Konstruktion und Gebrauch von Sprachbildern; Heidelberg: Carl Auer 1998 [Chicago 1980].

Landwehr, Achim: Historische Diskursanalyse; Frankfurt on the Main: Campus 2009.

Landwehr, Achim (ed.): Diskursiver Wandel; Wiesbaden: VS Verlag für Sozialwissenschaften 2010.

Lehnert, Gertrud / Kühl, Alicia / Weise, Katja (eds.): Modetheorie; Bielefeld: transcript 2014. https://doi.org/10.14361/transcript.9783839422502

Lichtenstein, Claude: "Der Designer als Interpret der Funktion", in: "Easy! Easy? Schweizer Industriedesign – das Büro M&E 1967–2002"; Zug: Museum Burg Zug 2002.

Linder, Marc / Saltzman, Charles L.: "A History of Medical Scientists on High Heels", in: International Journal of Health Services 28 (1998), pp. 201–225. https://doi.org/10.2190/ga2m-fla2-17fb-v5pe

Loos, Adolf: "das prinzip der bekleidung", in: Dietmar Rübel et al. (eds.): Materialästhetik. Quellentexte zu Kunst, Design und Architektur; Berlin: Reimer 2005, pp. 162–164.

Lutz, Raphael: "Die Verwissenschaftlichung des Sozialen als methodische und konzeptionelle Herausforderung für eine Sozialgeschichte des 20. Jahrhunderts", in: Geschichte und Gesellschaft 22 (1996), pp. 165–193.

LVR LandesMuseum Bonn: 1914. Welt in Farbe. Farbfotografie vor dem Krieg; Ostfildern: Hatje Cantz 2013.

Mareis, Claudia: Theorien des Designs zur Einführung; Hamburg: Junius 2014.

McNeil, Peter: "Conference Report 'The Future of Fashion Studies', University of Warwick April 30, 2009", in: Fashion Theory. The Journal of Dress, Body & Culture 14/1 (2010), pp. 105–110. https://doi.org/10.2752/175174110x12544983515312

McNeil, Peter / Riello, Giorgio: "Walking the Streets of London. Shoes in the Enlightenment", in: Giorgio Riello / Peter McNeil (eds.): Shoes. A History from Sandals to Sneakers; Oxford: Berg 2006, pp. 94–115.

McRobbie, Angela: In the culture society. Art, fashion and popular music; London: Routledge 1999.

Meili, Armin (ed.): Die Schweiz im Spiegel der Landesausstellung; Zürich 1940.

Mentges, Gabriele: "Die Angst vor der Uniformität", in: Gabriele Mentges / Birgit Richard (ed.): Schönheit der Uniformität. Körper, Kleidung, Medien; Frankfurt on the Main and New York: Campus 2005, pp. 17–42.

Mentges, Gabriele: "Die Angst der Forscher vor der Mode – oder das Dilemma einer Modeforschung im deutschsprachigen Raum", in: Gudrun M. König / Gabriele Mentges / Michael R. Müller (eds.): Die Wissenschaften der Mode; Bielefeld: transcript 2015, pp. 27–47. https://doi.org/10.14361/9783839422007

Mentges, Gabriele / Richard, Birgit (ed.): Schönheit der Uniformität. Körper, Kleidung, Medien; Frankfurt on the Main and New York: Campus 2005.

Mitteilungen der Bally-Schuhfabriken Aktiengesellschaft, 1927–1940.

Mitteilungen der Bally-Schuhfabriken AG Schönenwerd an ihr Personal, 1941–1957.

Mundt, Barbara: Metropolen machen Mode. Haute Couture der Zwanziger Jahre; Bestandskatalog von Mode der 20er Jahre im Kunstgewerbemuseum Berlin, Staatliche Museen Preußischer Kulturbesitz; Berlin: Reimer 1989[3].

Nahshon, Edna: Jews and Shoes; Oxford: Berg 2008. https://doi.org/10.2752/9781847887207

Plumpe, Werner: "Unternehmer – Fakten und Fiktionen", in: Werner Plumpe (ed.): Unternehmer – Fakten und Fiktionen. Historisch-biografische Studien; Munich: De Gruyter Oldenburg 2014, pp. 1–26. https://doi.org/10.1515/9783110443509-003

Polese, Francesca / Blaszczyk, Regina Lee: "Fashion Forward. The Business History of Fashion", in: Business History 54 (2012), pp. 6–9. https://doi.org/10.1080/00076791.2011.617206

Pressedienst der Schweizerischen Landesausstellung: Landesausstellung im Werden; Zürich 1939.

Riello, Giorgio: A Foot in the Past: Consumers, Producers and Footwear in the Long Eighteenth Century; Oxford: Oxford University Press 2006.

Scalabrin, Clauspeter (ed.): Pionier und Pfaffenschreck. Die Memoiren des Carl Franz Bally; Baden: hier + jetzt 2009.

Schlaepfer, Conrad A.: Der Film im Dienste der Wirtschaft; Thalwil: E. Oesch 1943.

Schleif, Nina: SchaufensterKunst; Berlin and New York: Böhlau 2004.

Schlittler, Anna-Brigitte / Tietze, Katharina (eds.): Über Schuhe. Zur Geschichte und Theorie der Fussbekleidung; Bielefeld: transcript 2016.

Schmelzer-Ziringer, Barbara: Mode Design Theorie; Stuttgart: UTB 2015.

Schmid, Walter: Die wirtschaftliche Entwicklung der C.F. Bally A.G. und der Bally Schuhfabriken A.G. in Schönenwerd mit besonderer Berücksichtigung des Exportproblems; Schönenwerd: W. Widmer-Stebler 1939.

Schmidt, Georg / von Grüningen, Berchtold / Mussard, Jean: Werkbund und Nachkriegszeit. Drei Vorträge gehalten an der Jahrestagung des Schweizerischen Werkbundes zu Basel im Herbst 1943; Basel: Holbein 1944.

Schulthess, Elsa: "Typen Schweizerischer Sportschuhe", in: Das Werk 15 (1928), pp. 21–24.

Schulze, Andreas: Goldleder zwischen 1500 und 1800. Herstellung und Erhaltung; Markkleeberg: Sax 2011.

Schwizerhüsli, 1919–1926.

Semmelhack, Elizabeth: Heights of Fashion. A History of the Elevated Shoe; Toronto and Pittsburgh: Periscope Publishing & Bata Shoe Museum 2008.

Simmel, Georg: "Berliner Kunstgewerbe-Ausstellung", in: Werner Jung (ed.): Georg Simmel. Vom Wesen der Moderne. Essays zur Philosophie und Ästhetik; Hamburg: Junius 1990, pp. 167–174.

Specker, Louis (ed.): Schlicht elegant – Mode der 20er Jahre; St. Gallen: Stiftung St. Galler Museen 2000. [Exhibition: Historisches und Völkerkundemuseum St. Gallen, 11.11.2000–29.4.2001]

Stämpfli, Regula: Mit der Schürze in die Landesverteidigung. Frauenemanzipation und Schweizer Militär 1914–1945; Zürich: Orell Füssli 2002.

Staudinger, Dora: "Die Frau als Konsumentin", in: Aktionskomitee der Petition betreffend die Einführung des Frauenstimmrechtes in der Schweiz (ed.): Zu der Frage der Einführung des Frauenstimm- und -wahlrechtes in der Schweiz; Bern: Büchler 1929, pp. 37f.

Steele, Valerie / Hill, Colleen (eds.): Shoe Obsession; New Haven: Yale University Press 2013. [Exhibition: The Fashion Institute of Technology, New York, 7.2.–13.4.2013]

Stirlin, Hermann R.: "Zu den Problemen der Schuhindustrie – und der Industrie im allgemeinen", in: Industrielle Organisation 12 (1943), pp. 76–81.

Streuli, Fritz: "Die Mode als industrielles Problem", in: Gesellschaft für Marktforschung (ed.): Industrielle Probleme der Mode; Zürich 1944, pp. 15–21.

Styles, John: "Manufacturing, consumption and design in eighteenth-century England", in: John Brewer / Roy Porter (eds.): Consumption and The World of Goods; London and New York: Routledge 1993, pp. 527–554.

Sudrow, Anne: Der Schuh im Nationalsozialismus. Eine Produktgeschichte im deutsch-britisch-amerikanischen Vergleich; Göttingen: Wallstein 2010.

Thomann, Klaus Dieter: "Die Grenzen medizinischer Volksbelehrung. Gesundheitsaufklärung und Schuhmode – von Pieter Camper bis in das 20. Jahrhundert", in: Würzburger medizinhistorische Mitteilungen 10 (1992), pp. 257–287.

Toggweiler, Jakob: Die Holding Company in der Schweiz; Zürich 1926.

Tomkowiak, Ingrid: "Disneys Märchenfilme", in: Regina Bendix / Ulrich Marzolph (eds.): Hören, Lesen, Sehen, Spüren. Märchenrezeption im europäischen Vergleich; Baltmannsweiler: Schneider Verlag Hohengehren, pp. 209–233.

Tramer, Vera: "Frau Mode hat sich [...] ihr neustes Sommerkleid zurecht gelegt". Der Modebegriff in den Mitteilungen über Textil-Industrie von 1894 bis 1913; Zürich 2014 [unpublished seminar paper, University of Zürich].

Trapp, Grete: "Das Modetheater und sein Drum und Dran", in: Julius Wagner (ed.): Festliche Landi; Zürich 1940, pp. 51–62.

Wagner, Julius (ed.): Das goldene Buch der LA; Zürich 1939.

Wagner, Julius (ed.): Festliche Landi; Zürich 1940.

Wagner, Monika: Das Material der Kunst. Eine andere Geschichte der Moderne; Munich: C.H.Beck 2001.

Wild, Roman: "Frau Mode ist launenhaft". Produktions- und Absatzstrategien der Basler Seidenbandindustrie, 1900–1930; Zürich 2010 [unpublished licentiate thesis, University of Zürich].

Wild, Roman: "Volksschuhe und Volkstücher zu Volkspreisen. Zur Bewirtschaftung lederner und textiler Bedarfsartikel in der Schweiz im Ersten Weltkrieg", in: Schweizerische Zeitschrift für Geschichte 63 (2013), pp. 428–452.

Wild, Roman: Auf Schritt und Tritt. Der schweizerische Schuhmarkt 1918–1948; Zürich: NZZ Libro 2019. https://doi.org/10.24894/978-3-03810-460-5

Wild, Roman: "Verbandssekretäre und die Bewilligungsgesetze der schweizerischen Schuhwirtschaft. Ein Beitrag zu den kommunikativen Vorräumen der Macht", in: Gisela Hürlimann / Anja Rathmann-Lutz / André Mach / Janick Marina Schaufelbuehl (eds.): Lobbying. Die Vorräume der Macht / Les antichambres du pouvoir; Zürich: Chronos [due for release].

Wolff, Irma: "Die Frau als Konsumentin", in: Archiv für Sozialwissenschaft und Sozialpolitik 34 (1912), pp. 893–904.

Wüthrich, Andreas: Erläuterungen über die rationelle Fussbekleidung; Bern: Verlag des Verfassers 1876.

Zimmermann, Charles: "Vom Sinn und Zweck der Schweizer Modewoche", in: Das Werk 30 (1943), pp. 312f.

Zuppinger, Mabel: "Das Modetheater", in: Armin Meili (ed.): Die Schweiz im Spiegel der Landesausstellung; Zürich 1940, pp. 173–179.

Bally

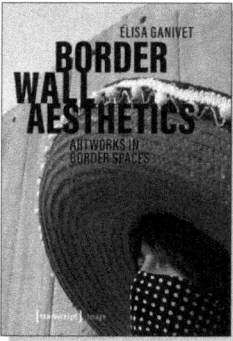

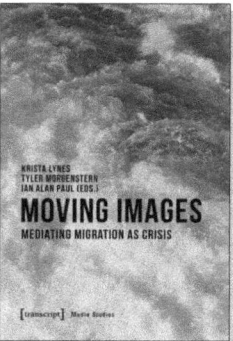

Cultural Studies

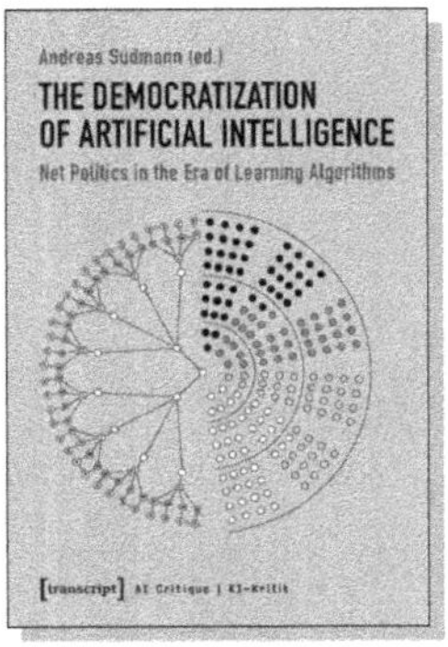

Andreas Sudmann (ed.)
The Democratization of Artificial Intelligence
Net Politics in the Era of Learning Algorithms

2019, 334 p., pb., col. ill.
49,99 € (DE), 978-3-8376-4719-8
E-Book: available as free open access publication
PDF: ISBN 978-3-8394-4719-2

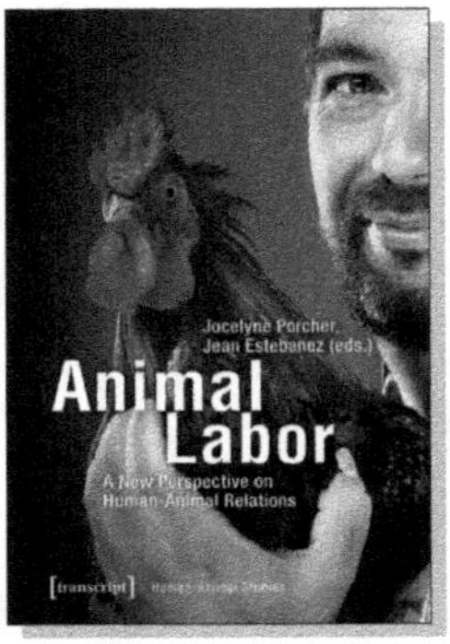

Jocelyne Porcher, Jean Estebanez (eds.)
Animal Labor
A New Perspective on Human-Animal Relations

2019, 182 p., hardcover
99,99 € (DE), 978-3-8376-4364-0
E-Book:
PDF: 99,99 € (DE), ISBN 978-3-8394-4364-4

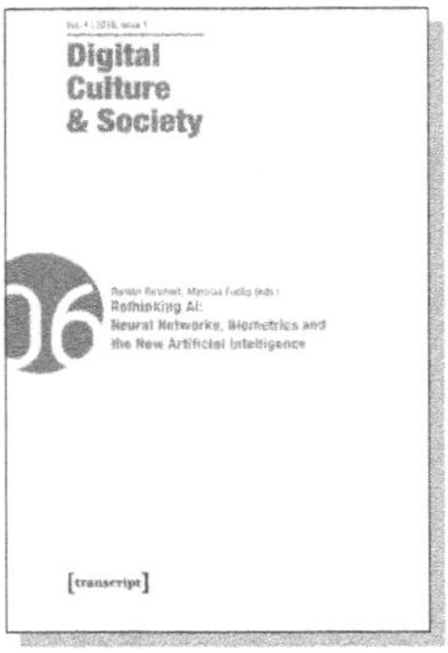

Ramón Reichert, Mathias Fuchs,
Pablo Abend, Annika Richterich, Karin Wenz (eds.)
Digital Culture & Society (DCS)
Vol. 4, Issue 1/2018 – Rethinking AI: Neural Networks, Biometrics and the New Artificial Intelligence

2018, 244 p., pb., ill.
29,99 € (DE), 978-3-8376-4266-7
E-Book:
PDF: 29,99 € (DE), ISBN 978-3-8394-4266-1

All print, e-book and open access versions of the titles in our list are available in our online shop www.transcript-publishing.com

GPSR Authorized Representative: Easy Access System Europe, Mustamäe tee 50, 10621 Tallinn, Estonia, gpsr.requests@easproject.com

www.ingramcontent.com/pod-product-compliance
Lightning Source LLC
Chambersburg PA
CBHW070110030426
42335CB00016B/2092
* 9 7 8 3 8 3 7 6 5 7 3 8 8 *